Ending The Abortion Debate:

On The Issues That Truly Matter

Table of Contents

Introduction..1-14

Chapter 1: Notable Statistical Trends on Abortion: Poverty, Affluence, and Income Inequality...15-63

Chapter 2: Notable Statistical Trends on Abortion: Domestic Violence and Related Issues
....64-77

Chapter 3: What Can Be Done...................78-105

Chapter 4: Why The Debate is Irrelevant: Pro-life, Pro-Choice, and a Synthesis... 106-123

Chapter 5: Why a Fetus is Not a Person and Should Not Have Legal Rights.. 124-142

Conclusion..143-152

Introduction

Prior to laying down some groundwork and discussing the central thesis, it would be useful to go over the reasons why the book is formatted the way it is. Each chapter has been designed to ensure that all citations are accessible to the average reader. Despite the fact that most citations are less formal, the sources draw from more formal citations. The issue with the usual academic citations and why I decided to avoid using them when communicating to a general and layman audience is because formal citations — namely those found in journals and publications — are usually veiled behind a paywall. A work like this should make a good attempt at distinguishing itself from works written in the ivory high towers of academia. My intent is not to alienate my audience, but to draw it closer to the important issues this work will focus on. Citations will be shown as footnotes at the bottom of each page and the links to each webpage will also be provided.

The data and facts that will be discussed are crucial to the thesis. They provide integral support to a crux that not everyone will be initially persuaded of. That is the point of engaging these topics in the way in which I am doing now. In my experience, there is resistance for reasons that I will discuss shortly. Given that, the sources referenced have to be accessible and this, for the sake of maintaining transparency for the more skeptical members of the audience. It should be kept in mind that much more work has to be done in order to dissuade someone that a position they identify with is erred than to convince them to subscribe to a different position.

The primary reason for writing this work is that I strongly believe I argue in favor of the most viable position, one that is defined by a series of actionable solutions to the issues confronting women who choose to terminate their pregnancies. The point is not to simply end the abortion debate and offer no new ground to tread. It is not that I have become so exhausted by the hard work of having a debate on these matters that I see it as simpler to just do away with the dialogue altogether, but rather that after years of discussing the politics and ethics of abortion, I have come to the realization that the debate itself is not important. Such a realization is not the consensus. As such, there are quite a number of people that need to be convinced of this realization and the solutions I will be offering and defending. While it is true that most of these individuals are pro-lifers, there are also pro-choicers who need to lay down their weapons, per se. This work does not ask pro-lifers to concede. This work attempts to arrange an armistice.

    One of the pivotal questions I attempt to answer is whether the abortion debate really matters. To answer this question, the reasons women choose to have an abortion must be taken into consideration. People tend to lose sight of these reasons when arguing about the politics and ethics of abortion. It will be demonstrated that if one intends to mitigate or put an end to something, one can do so by focusing on its precursors. While pro-lifers and pro-choicers cannot find much common ground, I will identify a location for all sides to come together. Reducing abortion is a worthwhile goal and since most pro-choicers may need to be persuaded of that, it is therefore a worthwhile task that will be met later. Pro-lifers, on the other hand, have communicated that they prefer to put an end to abortion altogether. Whichever the goal is, be it to reduce the occurrence of something or to put an end to it altogether, the same steps have to be taken. This is fertile soil for all sides to plant seeds.

    A pro-choicer does not have to agree with a pro-lifer's reasons for wanting to put an end to abortion. She only has to agree with the conclusion that targeting the precursors of abortion is a valuable endeavor in and of itself. The decision to have an abortion is often due to multifarious reasons. Among these reasons are the fact that the woman in question cannot afford to raise a child, having a baby would dramatically change her life, she does not want to be a single mom or she is experiencing issues in her relationship.[1] The first of these reasons is important because it leads to a problem people, whether pro-lifer or pro-choicer, should be concerned about: poverty. The poverty rate among children in the United States was 19.9% in 2013 and has been steadily declining since.[2] As of 2016, the poverty rate among children is 18%, which is still too high.[3] Though abortion rates in 2017 were at their lowest in the United States, the abortion rate among poor women increased. This is a trend that holds year after

---

[1] Finer, Lawrence B., et. al. "Reasons U.S. Women Have Abortions: Quantitative and Qualitative Perspectives". *Guttmacher Institute*. ND. Web. 21 Nov 2014. <https://www.guttmacher.org/journals/psrh/2005/reasons-us-women-have-abortions-quantitative-and-qualitative-perspectives>

[2] Baldari, Cara. "A Snapshot of Children in Poverty". *First Focus*. 14 Sep 2014. Web. 14 Oct 2017. <https://firstfocus.org/resources/fact-sheet/snapshot-children-poverty-2013>

[3] "Child Poverty in America 2016: National Analysis". Children's Defense Fund. 9 Sep 2017. Web. 7 Oct 2017. <http://www.childrensdefense.org/reports/>

year.[4] If so many children are currently in poverty, one has to wonder whether it can be expected that the mothers of those children will continue a new pregnancy in all cases. It is only reasonable that some of them will choose to have an abortion.

    This inevitably leads to a related issue worth addressing. If one cannot afford a child at the moment, one should do everything in one's power to prevent pregnancy in the first place. As statistics have shown, abortion decreases with age in the United States, particularly after the age of 19; put another way, abortion rates are higher among younger women.[5] This suggests an educational or literacy problem. More sex education might be necessary. More preventative measures need to be available so that abortion rates continue to decrease.

---

[4] Boonstra, Heather D.. "Abortion in the Lives of Women Struggling Financially: Why Insurance Coverage Matters". Guttmacher Institute. 14 July 2016. Web. 7 Oct 2017. <https://www.guttmacher.org/gpr/2016/07/abortion-lives-women-struggling-financially-why-insurance-coverage-matters>

[5] Ibid. [1]

This is a worthwhile goal no matter what one's personal motives are.

Then there are relationship issues, domestic violence in particular. It cannot be expected of a woman to want to carry the child of an abusive significant other. Given that this is a problem according to statistics taken year after year, domestic violence should be more of a focal point. This is, no doubt, more difficult to address than the previous issue. Providing sex education is one thing, but convincing abusive men that violence against their partners is wrong seems to be a more daunting task.

Abusive men are not made overnight. There is obviously something that needs to be addressed in overall male psychology.[6] There is perhaps something to be said about psychopathy being more prevalent in males. This aggressive wiring has all to do with genetics, specifically in receiving one x-chromosome

---

[6] Arkowitz, Hal. "Are Men the More Belligerent Sex?". *Scientific American*. 1 Apr 2010. Web. 21 Nov 2014. <http://www.scientificamerican.com/article/are-men-the-more-belligerent-sex/>

from the mother.⁷ The *nature* side of this aggressive wiring in some men is one thing, the *nurture* side of it is another, so it is not the x-chromosome on its own, but also a litany of background experiences in the lives of these men. This would require taking therapeutic measures that are not always available. Regardless, this is something that requires time to figure out.

    This is why I will argue that the abortion debate does not matter at all. I will make clear that the moral status of a fetus, potentiality, shared value, reductionism, and non-reductionism are merely smokescreens. There are real issues behind the plumes that require attention. It will be demonstrated that limiting abortion by focusing on its precursors is a worthwhile goal. Whether one sees it as a worthwhile goal because of the inherent value in addressing factors like poverty and domestic violence or because one desires to put an end to abortion does not matter. In other words, one's religious, political,

---

[7] Hunter, Philip. "The Psycho Gene". *EMBO Reports* 11.9 (2010): 667–669. *PMC*. Web. 7 Oct. 2017. <https://www.ncbi.nlm.nih.gov/pmc/articles/PMC2933872/>

or personal motives for wanting to act against the precursors of abortion make no difference.

This is where all sides can work together. This is where pro-choicers, pro-lifers, and anyone in-between can meet to solve the issues related to choosing to have an abortion once and for all. Reducing abortion is periphery to and yet the inevitable consequence of finding a way to address male psychology and domestic abuse, poverty, lack of jobs, income inequality, and sex education or general illiteracy. This will thus make a far bigger impact and leave a deeper imprint; families will benefit more, abortion will be reduced, and more importantly, babies will be born into self-sufficient households. The arguments, whether for or against abortion, lose all priority when considering these issues. I can only hope to convince you of this in the upcoming chapters. What follows is an overview of how each chapter is organized.

In the first chapter, I will flesh out important statistical trends concerning poverty, affluence, income disparity, and related issues. Specifically, the trends presented will serve as indicators of deeper issues. For example, there is a startling increase in abortions among women falling below the poverty line in the United States. For women above the poverty line, the trend is precisely the opposite. These trends will be compared to trends around the world and put into a larger context that will be the focus of the chapter's discussion.

I will discuss, for instance, the longterm effects restrictive abortion policies have on women and their families. Connections will be made between higher poverty rates versus how restrictive or permissive a given country's abortion policies are. It will be made clear that poverty, like wealth, is kept in the family, so to speak. Poverty, to put it another way, is inherited and in countries with stricter abortion policies, trends in poverty rates persist with little to no change. The discussion on poverty will be conjoined to the discussion on how a lack of educational and career opportunities allow for these trends to persist.

The second chapter will focus on domestic violence and related issues in relationships. It will prove useful to explain why domestic violence is overlooked as a precursor to abortion. It will be shown that salient connections can be made between domestic violence and relationship problems, especially in light of statistics concerning poverty and single-parent households. I will also discuss how domestic violence can become an issue after a woman has an abortion. The assumption here is that there were already tensions that prevented a woman from telling her partner that she made the often difficult choice to have an abortion.

The third chapter will propose solutions by addressing the question of what can be done. In elaborating on the connection between poverty and lack of educational and career opportunities, it will be shown that increased opportunities result in reducing poverty rates. There are historical arguments to this effect, but there are also modern-day examples one could focus on. Religious extremists in parts of the Muslim World, for example, prohibit young girls from pursuing an education.[8][9] Whether or not such a prohibition has any effect on the poverty rates in such countries will be explored in the first chapter; the third chapter will then show what has happened in places where such prohibitions on education and the pursuit of certain career paths were lifted, and how the implementation of similar solutions will alleviate current circumstances.

When confronted by the pressing nature of the issues that will be discussed and how they lead women to choose abortion, the conclusion I am hoping to convince readers of is that the ongoing debate should be considered insignificant. What will become important are methods by which proposed solutions can be carried out. What will also become important will be the alleviation of the precursors of

---

[8] Popalzai, Masoud. "Afghanistan: Men throw acid into girls' faces for 'going to school'". *CNN*. 5 Jul 2015. Web. 22 Oct 2017. <https://www.cnn.com/2015/07/04/asia/afghanistan-schoolgirls-acid-attack/index.html>

[9] Torgan, Allie. "Acid attacks, poison: What Afghan girls risk by going to school". *CNN*. 17 Mar 2016. Web. 22 Oct 2017. <https://www.cnn.com/2012/08/02/world/meast/cnnheroes-jan-afghan-school/index.html>

abortion. It will also be clear that there is no other position that does better. Reducing abortion rates inevitably involves alleviating the precursors of abortion. This will be much of the focus of the third chapter, along with a discussion of other reasons why the abortion debate is not important in the fourth chapter. There is, for instance, a tendency for people to double down on their stance when confronted. In some cases, there may be no way around such a proclivity, hence making a debate not only insignificant but futile.

Finally, chapter five will clarify an allusion I will make throughout. The abortion debate is not even important when discussing personhood in relation to the moral status of a fetus. The more skeptical reader will wonder why and for sake of clarification and not of argument, I will present reasons as to why I do not regard that discussion as important. There should not be a delay in action given the assumption that a fetus is a person, potential or actual. If anything, should one's motivation be to reduce abortion rates because one believes a fetus is a person, one should be more inclined to meet me at the common ground and work on alleviating the precursors of abortion. In any case, one should not stop working to provide relief to women and their families to argue over the moral status of a fetus. Within the scope of the overall discussion, this chapter will serve as an appendix to chapter four. It will be further evidence that the debate does not matter. What really matters is the impact that can be made, work that carries a palpable weight of moral obligation.

1
Notable Statistical Trends on Abortion: Poverty, Affluence, and Income Inequality

For the purpose of making this presentation easier to follow, the issues discussed over the next two chapters will be grouped together according to the relevance. In other words, I will present and interpret statistics and trends on poverty, affluence, and income disparity, and elaborate on each of these issues to make clear the connection each has to the decision to have an abortion. I will touch on how the level of one's education and the career opportunities one has helped to determine one's level of income and therefore, whether one is affluent or in poverty.

As mentioned earlier, wherever one stands on the question of abortion, poverty deserves one's attention. Poverty rates among children were briefly touched on earlier, but to make clear the gravity of the issue of poverty, it is imperative to present year-to-year trends rather than the statistics pertaining to a particular year. In this way, both the progress made with regards to poverty and further progress to be made is made manifest. Moreover, since abortion is not an exclusively American issue, the statistical trends will not be limited to the United States. I will draw from statistics taken in advanced, developing, and less advanced countries, so that prognoses in the countries discussed become clear. The situation, as it relates to poverty and the other issues I will discuss, will differ from country to country and as such, women in some countries find themselves further from self-sufficiency, equality, and financial stability.

    Though Michael New makes the following observation to serve another purpose, his perspective is pivotal to understanding the connection between abortion and poverty. New observed that "many of the countries where abortion is legally restricted tend to have high poverty rates and a variety of other social pathologies that increase the demand for abortions."[10] Implicit in his statement is that high

---

[10] Doucleff, Michaeleen. "What Drives Abortion: The Law Or Income?". *NPR*. 28 Sep 2014. Web. 8 Oct 2017. <https://www.npr.org/sections/goatsandsoda/2014/09/28/349890020/what-drives-abortion-the-law-or-income>

poverty rates are related to an increased demand for abortions. Statistical trends support the conclusion that abortion rates are higher when poverty rates are high. What follows will be a presentation of statistics in advanced countries, developing countries, and less advanced countries. Since there is already a disparity between the affluence found in a developed country and that in a less advanced country, one can reasonably expect to see higher abortion rates in countries where populations are less affluent and more impoverished.

Poverty and Abortion in the United States: A Brief Overview

Information derived from a Guttmacher analysis that monitored changes in the characteristics of abortion patients from 2008 to 2014 was used to inform the following infographic[11]:

---

11 Jerman J, Jones RK and Onda T, <u>Characteristics of U.S. Abortion Patients in 2014 and Changes Since 2008</u>, New York: Guttmacher Institute, 2016. <<u>https://www.guttmacher.org/report/characteristics-us-abortion-patients-2014</u>>

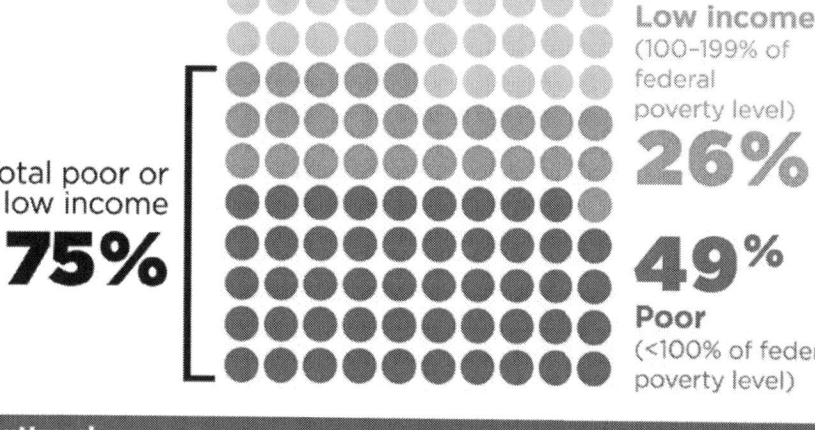

That 49% of women having abortions in the United States in 2014 were women falling below the poverty line is a striking statistic, but the trend since 2008 is of greater importance. Briefly, in 2014, a family of two with a household income of $15,730 or less was considered poor or in other words, a family that fell below the poverty line. In 2008, 42% of women having abortions were women who fell below the poverty line. The trend yields an increase in abortion rates in women below the poverty line of ~16.7% over that seven-year span or ~2.3% per year.[12] The trend continuing as such resulted in an increase in abortion rates of ~50% in women below the federal poverty line in the year 2017.[13]

The trend among affluent women in the United States is precisely the opposite. 31% of women choosing to have an abortion were in the highest income groups in 2008. In 2014, that number decreased to 25%. This yields a decrease of ~19.4%

---

[12] [(0.49 - 0.42)/0.42] x 100 = 16.7% over seven years; 0.167/7 x 100 = 2.4% per year

[13] [0.49 + (0.49 x 0.024)] x 100 = 50%

over that period or ~2.8% per year.[14] Of course, there are nuances to consider, reasons explaining why these trends persist.

One underlying factor is child poverty. As mentioned earlier, child poverty in the United States decreased from 19.9% to 18% over a three year period, which yields a decrease of ~5.7% over that three year period. The sharpest decline happened between 2015 and 2016; child poverty decreased by 8.6% in that time. To put the numbers in context, over 13 million children are living in poverty in the United States and close to half that number are living in extreme poverty.[15] The statistics are comparable in the next two cases I want to focus on. The task now is to keep these figures present in one's mind. While the figures themselves are of importance, the underlying reasons for the persistence of these trends are of greater importance

---

[14] [(0.25 - 0.31)/0.31] x 100 = -19.4% over seven years; .24/7 x 100 = -2.8% per year

[15] "Child Poverty in America 2016: National Analysis". *Children's Defense Fund.* 18 Sep 2017. Web. 14 Oct 2017. <https://www.childrensdefense.org/reports/>

Despite the differences between abortion policies in the United States and Northern Ireland, poverty rates in Northern Ireland are strikingly similar to those in the US. Another area of interest in the United Kingdom is London. Both areas clue one into the palpable connection between abortion and poverty. Not only does poverty influence a woman's decision to have an abortion, restricting abortion rights all but guarantees that her descendants remain in poverty. Though being part of the UK, Northern Ireland had stricter laws than the rest of the region. Prior to examining these two cases in the UK, it is necessary to understand why the policies in Northern Ireland differed from those in England, Scotland, and Wales.

Poverty and Abortion in Northern Ireland: A Brief Overview

For starters, the 1967 Abortion Act that legalized abortion in the UK did not apply to Northern Ireland. Instead, Northern Ireland operated under the 1861 Offenses Against the Person Act. This act prohibited abortion. Northern Ireland amended the act in 1929, 1938, and again in 1945. The 1929 Infant Life Act and the 1938 Bourne Judgment made abortion permissible provided that there is a risk to the would-be mother's physical or mental health. The 1945 Criminal Justice Act made it so that having an abortion is treated as murder, hence imposing the threat of a life sentence.[16] When the 1967 Abortion Act was passed, the UK had not taken control of Northern Ireland; though this would happen five years later, abortion rights were not extended to women in Northern Ireland. Briefly, UK's Westminster government may devolve certain matters to the Northern Ireland Assembly, which was created in the 1998 Belfast Agreement. In 2010, abortion policy was devolved to Belfast, hence the Northern Ireland Assembly's strict policies on abortion.[17]

---

[16] Louise-Connolly, Marie. "NI women not entitled to free NHS abortions in England says High Court". *BBC*. 8 May 2014. Web. 14 Oct 2017. <https://www.bbc.com/news/business-27325363>

[17] Annapragada, Akshaya. "No Choice in Belfast". *Harvard Political Review*. 14 Sep 2016. Print. 14 Oct 2017.

While the number of abortions in the US are in the hundreds of thousands every year, the number of abortions in Northern Ireland are in the hundreds. If considering the fact that there were over 640,000 abortions in the US in 2013 versus only 724 in Northern Ireland in the year 2016, one would scoff at comparing these two cases.[18][19][20] What is being compared is not the number of induced abortions, but rather the influence poverty has in both cases. Child poverty in Northern Ireland is proportionately higher than in the US; 25% of children are in poverty.[21] This means that their families fall below Northern

---

[18] NA. "Abortion Fast Facts". *CNN*. 28 May 2017. Web. 22 Oct 2017. <https://gantdaily.com/2015/05/20/abortion-fast-facts/>

[19] Gentleman, Amelia. "Abortion figures prompt fresh calls for reform of Northern Irish law". *The Guardian*. 13 Jun 2017. Web. 22 Oct 2017. <https://www.theguardian.com/uk-news/2017/jun/13/abortion-figures-prompt-fresh-calls-for-reform-of-northern-irish-law>

[20] From Gentleman's article: "The number of women traveling from Northern Ireland to England for an abortion fell slightly last year to 724, from 833 in 2015"

[21] Miller, Claire. "A quarter of Northern Ireland children living in poverty". *Belfast Live*. 1 Oct 2016. Web. 22 Oct 2017. <https://www.belfastlive.co.uk/news/belfast-news/quarter-northern-ireland-children-living-11960842>

Ireland's poverty line of £21,900 per year., which is the average median household income. What also stands out about child poverty in Northern Ireland is the fact that it is steadily increasing year after year. Child poverty increased by 8.7% from 2014 to 2015 — up to 25% from 23%.[22] As stated earlier, some women find themselves further from financial stability and security; they also find themselves further from securing rights and Northern Ireland is precisely such a case.

So pronounced is the influence of living in poverty on women choosing to have abortions in Northern Ireland that it is brought up by opponents of abortion in Northern Ireland's Assembly. Peter Bottomley, a conservative legislator, stated that "only the poor should be denied lawful abortions."[23] Angela Jackman, an attorney who represented a 17-year-old seeking an abortion, asked: "what are women in

---

[22] Ibid. [21]

[23] Castle, Stephen. "U.K. to Fund Abortions in England for Women From Northern Ireland". *The New York Times*. 29 Jun 2017. Web. 22 Oct 2017. <https://www.nytimes.com/2017/06/29/world/europe/uk-abortions-england-northern-ireland.html>

Northern Ireland who need terminations supposed to do if they cannot afford to pay privately for the service in England?"[24] The financial burden on these women is a cause for concern. As Ann Furedi, chief executive of the British Pregnancy Advisory Service stated: "Outlawing abortion does not prevent women from having abortions, it simply increases the physical, financial and emotional burden of obtaining the care they need."[25]

In a country where there is a larger religious population — roughly 83% of the population — more insidious factors have to explain bypassing even deeply held religious convictions and making a decision to have an abortion.[26] In Northern Ireland's case, the key variable is child poverty. When 25% of children are in poverty, more than 100,000 children to

---

[24] NA. "NI women not entitled to free NHS abortions in England says High Court". *BBC*. 8 May 2014. Web. 22 Oct 2017. <https://www.bbc.com/news/business-27325363>

[25] Ibid. [24]

[26] Sedghi, Ami. "Northern Ireland census 2011: religion and identity mapped". *The Guardian*. 12 Dec 2012. Web. 22 Oct 2017. <https://www.theguardian.com/news/datablog/2012/dec/12/northern-ireland-census-2011-religion-identity-mapped>

be exact, the choice to have another child would have a physical, psychological, and financial impact on a woman and her family. As an anonymous woman going by the name of Lauren explained, "I was suffering from post-natal depression after giving birth to my son when I became pregnant again. I knew that mentally, emotionally and financially I couldn't cope with another child."[27]

Poverty and Abortion in London: A Brief Overview

The situation in London is not much better despite looser abortion laws. While the poverty rate in England is ~20%, the poverty rate in the capital city

---

[27] Fenton, Siobhan. "The UK's abortion shame: Northern Ireland urged to stop prosecuting women under abortion ban". *Independent.* 10 Apr 2016. Web. 22 Oct 2017. <https://www.independent.co.uk/news/uk/home-news/uk-s-abortion-shame-northern-ireland-urged-stop-prosecuting-women-under-abortion-ban-a6975441.html>

of London is ~27%.[28] Again, the higher the rate of poverty, the higher the rate of abortions. Similar to the situations in the US and Northern Ireland, nine of the ten areas in England with the highest number of abortions are boroughs in London.[29] Also similar to the cases surveyed thus far, London has a child poverty rate that is well above the national average of ~31%. Roughly 41% of children are in poverty in London; 20% are in extreme poverty. That amounts to approximately 650,000 children.[30]

For all that has been said before of child poverty, the palpable connection these rates have to a woman's decision to have an abortion has not been demonstrated. This, however, is unfortunately simple to show. In the cases thus far surveyed, there are links

---

[28] Hill, Dave. "Number of London's 'working poor' surges 70% in 10 years". *The Guardian*. 20 Oct 2015. Web. 22 Oct 2017. <https://www.personneltoday.com/hr/articles/number-of-londons-working-poor-surges-70-in-10-years/>

[29] "Abortion rates show regional variations". *BBC*. 19 May 2016. Web. 22 Oct 2017. <https://www.bbc.com/news/uk-england-36321484>

[30] Farthing, Rys. "Health, Inequality and Child Poverty in London". *London Journal of Primary Care* 3.1 (2010): 2–4. Print. <https://www.ncbi.nlm.nih.gov/pmc/articles/PMC3960686/>

between child poverty and the likelihood of poor dental health, low birth weight, accidents, disability, and infant mortality.

In London, for instance, children born into poor families are two times as likely to die at birth or during infancy than children born into more affluent families and are also two times more likely to develop cerebral palsy as children in the wealthiest one-fifth. It is 19% likelier that these children have poor dental health and 9% more likely that they are of low birth weight.[31] In a series of longitudinal studies conducted by the University of London, it was shown that not only are disabled children more likely to be economically disadvantaged, but also this disadvantage may increase with age relative to the kind of disability the child has. As Parsons and Platt explain:

The socio-economic profile at 9 months shows that children with a disability, however and whenever defined, are more likely to be born into disadvantage. This provides further support to

---

[31] Ibid. [30]

the growing body of evidence that shows childhood disability to be firmly associated with disadvantaged family circumstances.[32]

This is as true in England as it is in London. These factors are also present in Northern Ireland.

In Northern Ireland, there were five deaths per one thousand births; this represents the highest rate of infant mortality in the UK.[33] As Freeman noted:

> Children in Northern Ireland who come from low-income households and attend disadvantaged schools (as classified by the proportion of children entitled to free school meals) have more dental caries, consume foods higher in sugars and fats, and are more likely to eat candy and sugar-based drinks at break-time than other children.[34]

---

[32] Hills, J. (Chair), Brewer, M., Jenkins, S., Lister, R., Lupton, R., Machin, S., Mills, C., Modood, T., Rees, T., Riddell, S. 2010. An anatomy of economic inequality in the UK:Report of the National Equality Panel. London: Government Equalities Office.

[33] Smyth Catherine. "Northern Ireland child health 'among worst in W Europe'". 15 Jun 2017. Web. 22 Oct 2017. <https://www.bbc.com/news/uk-northern-ireland-40278243>

[34] Freeman, R., Oliver, M., Bunting, G., Kirk, J. and Saunderson, W. (2001): Addressing children's oral health inequalities in Northern Ireland: a research-practice-community partnership initiative. Public Health Reports. 116, 617-625.

This explains the higher rates of childhood obesity in the UK as well. Poverty results in poor physical and mental health and puts added stress on low-income families. This is precisely why studies making this link also focus on the prevalence of nicotine and alcohol use among parents in low-income households.[35]

Rather than tread over these old coals as they would pertain to the United States, it is time now to survey a developing country. Prior to doing so, it must be stressed that a more exhaustive cross-country analysis is not necessary to prove that poverty weighs heavily on a woman's decision to have an abortion. All that is necessary is showing that no matter the stage of a country's development and no matter the income disparities that exist in a given country, poverty is inherently linked to higher abortion rates. In the three cases surveyed thus far, the connection has proven salient. Moreover, while there are proportional differences in the number of induced

---

[35] Ibid. [33]

abortions on a case by case basis — with the US, for instance, having a much higher number of abortions per year when compared to Northern Ireland — the prevalent and recurring concomitant of high abortion rates in each case is high poverty rates.

Poverty and Abortion in Brazil: A Brief Overview

Of all the cases surveyed, Brazil will prove the most interesting because of the progress the country has made in eliminating extreme poverty. Brazil still faces the problem of relative poverty, which is best identified by comparing income level versus the minimum amount of income necessary to meet the standard of living in a given area or country, i.e., livable income. As of 2009, Brazil's poverty rate was 21.9%, which is comparable to the US, London, and Northern Ireland.[36] This is down from 35.8% in 2003,

---

[36] Guedes, Gilvan R. et al. "Poverty and Inequality in the Rural Brazilian Amazon: A Multidimensional Approach." *Human ecology: an interdisciplinary journal* 40.1 (2012): 41–57. *PMC.* Web. 22 Oct. 2017.

which makes for a 38.8% decline in seven years.[37] This is by far the steepest decline of the four countries we have looked at. In chapter three, when proposing solutions, Brazil will prove exemplary with respect to what needs to be done to solve the problem of poverty.

Despite these strides, child poverty has been consistently higher than poverty all because as Fernandez explains, "rates of poverty among children greatly exceeded poverty rates among older persons" because "of the age bias in social policy associated with the Bismarckian approach. Transfers were focused on old age as opposed to families and children."[38] Briefly, the assumption is that the paternalism inherent to the Bismarckian approach applies better to the elderly than it does to children and their families because younger patients are

---

[37] Sabry, Sarah. "How did Brazil reduce poverty and inequality?". *Madamasr*. Web. 21 Jan 2016. Web. 22 Oct 2017. <https://www.madamasr.com/en/2016/01/21/opinion/economy/how-did-brazil-reduce-poverty-and-inequality/>

[38] Fernandez, Elizabeth, et al. Theoretical and empirical insights into child and family poverty: cross national perspectives. Springer, 2015. 161. Print.

likelier to exercise autonomy. Older and frailer patients cannot take care of themselves. They do not have the energy, presence of mind, and/or money to live life as they see fit. Autonomy, especially when defined as the capacity to pursue one's happiness, predetermines as paternalistic any attempt to take care of older patients. As Agich goes on to conclude, "the diminished capacity that brings elders into long-term care contributes to the view that dependence entails subservience and inferiority; but if independence is only, or primarily, valued, then we should not be surprised to find that responding even to basic human needs is fraught with contradiction.[39] This Bismarckian emphasis on social welfare readily explains why the child poverty rate for children under the age of fourteen is ~40%. That percentage represents 17 million children. 5.8 million out of these 17 million children are in extreme poverty.[40]

---

[39] Agich GJ: Dependence and Autonomy in Old Age. 2003, University Press, Cambridge

[40] "Forty Percent of Children Under 14 Live in Poverty in Brazil". *Rio Times*. 21 Mar 2017. Web. 22 Oct 2017. <https://riotimesonline.com/brazil-news/rio-politics/forty-percent-of-children-under-14-live-in-poverty-in-brazil/>

Once again, these familial poverty rates translate to higher abortion rates. When coupled with Brazil's strict laws prohibiting abortions, the rates are shown to be even higher. Not surprisingly, Yury Puello Orozco, director of Catholics for the Right to Choose, relays the following: "The majority of women who are at risk from abortions are black, poor, uneducated and live in the marginal neighborhoods."[41] She also explains that about 20% of women have had unsafe abortions, so this now represents a public health issue.

Though Brazil proves exemplary in the manner in which it has reduced poverty, the country's strict abortion policies are a shot in the foot. Stricter abortion policies come at a cost and that cost is losing the lives of women, persons whose moral status is not arguable. In other words, women are undeniably persons and even the most conservative pro-lifer does not argue against that conclusion. If

---

[41] Navarro-Garcia, Lulu. "Brazil's Restrictions On Abortion May Get More Restrictive". *NPR*. 28 Oct 2013. Web. 22 Oct 2017. <https://www.npr.org/sections/parallels/2013/10/29/241410709/brazils-restrictions-on-abortion-may-get-more-restrictive>

the loss of a fetus' life is of importance to any of my readers, then it should follow that the loss of a woman's life due to complications from unsafe abortions is also of importance.

As an obstetrician in Pernambuco explains: "I have followed cases of women with very serious infections due to unsafe abortions that had septic shock and died."[42] She goes on to describe treating patients with ruptured uteruses and infections in their abdominal cavity resulting from inducing abortions themselves. What makes this a public health concern is that there were roughly 500,000 abortions in 2015 in Brazil. That number remained relatively stable in 2016. Not surprisingly, the less educated and impoverished women accounted for most of the country's induced abortions in both years.[43] Given this, that Brazil is counteracting its

---

[42] Wurth, Margaret. "Why Brazil Should Decriminalize Abortion". *Human Rights Watch*. 28 Sep 2017. Web. 25 Nov 2017. <https://www.hrw.org/news/2017/09/28/why-brazil-should-decriminalize-abortion>

[43] Debora Diniz &, Marcelo Medeiros &, Alberto Madeiro. (2017). National Abortion Survey 2016. Ciência & Saúde Coletiva. 22. 653-660. 10.1590/1413-81232017222.23812016.

own attempts to reduce poverty is no illusion. While Brazil is making strides to reduce poverty, policies that make the countries previously discussed pale by comparison, the country's strict abortion policies are slowing the progress made and putting women's health and lives at risk.

This pattern repeats itself in countries where abortion policies are strict. I will focus on three regions to show conclusively that stricter laws do not reduce abortions. What stricter laws do is reduce abortions on the books, which is to say abortions that are officially reported; it does not, however, reduce abortions under the table. As in Brazil's case, more women are resorting to taking pills to terminate an unwanted pregnancy.[44]

Poverty and Abortion in Chile: A Brief Overview

Due to its proximity to Brazil, Chile proves to be an interesting case study. For much of recent history, Chile's abortion laws have been among the

---

[44] Ibid. [42]

most restrictive in South America, if not, the entire world. For perspective, in 2013, Chilean President Sebastián Piñera praised an 11-year-old girl who was raped by her step-father for carrying her child to full term. Piñera said: "She's 14 weeks pregnant and yesterday she surprised us all with words showing depth and maturity, when she said that despite the pain caused by the man who raped her, she wanted to have and take care of her baby."[45] Support for such draconian laws goes back to Augusto Pinochet, who imposed these restrictive laws in 1989. Like Brazil, Chile's strides in reducing poverty have been set back by restrictive abortion laws.

Despite these laws, there are still approximately 160,000 abortions per year. These unsafe abortions accounted for 25% of maternal mortality in 2004.[46] Of these 160,000 abortions, about

---

[45] NA. "Chilean president praises raped girl, 11, for going through with pregnancy". *The Guardian*. 9 Jul 2013. Web. 4 Dec 2018.<https://www.theguardian.com/world/2013/jul/10/chilean-president-praises-raped-pregnancy>

[46] "Abortion in Chile". *Human Rights Watch*. ND. Web. 4 Dec 2018. <https://www.ncbi.nlm.nih.gov/pmc/articles/PMC6927382/>

64,000 were performed on minors.[47] As is the case in every country having strict abortion laws, poor women turn to unsafe methods in order to have an abortion. In Chile, if medication cannot be purchased on the internet or if a woman cannot find a cheap and illegal provider, they have to find a way to travel to northern Peru to have an abortion. This should already sound extremely familiar given that many women in Northern Ireland traveled to England to undergo their procedures. Similarly, this puts a financial strain on women already in poverty.

 Though there are no statistics on how common it is for a Chilean woman to travel to Peru to get an abortion, Freeman writes that she "spoke to healthcare practitioners who all believed it to be common." She "managed to speak to one young woman who travelled across the border when she accidentally fell pregnant. She saw Peru as an opportunity to find the future she wanted but was

---

[47] Freeman, Cordelia. "Chile: the long road to abortion reform". *The Conversation*. 25 Aug 2017. Web. 4 Dec 2018. <https://www.independent.co.uk/news/world/politics/chile-the-long-road-to-abortion-reform-a7917791.html>

frightened all the same, knowing that she could face up to five years in prison if she was caught."[48] Freeman goes on to explain that these procedures are hit or miss. Though some of the clinics are run by licensed physicians specializing in abortions, others are run by people with no training or qualifications.

Though the situation in Chile is not unique given how unfortunately typical restrictive abortion laws are around the world, the laws were in place long enough for one to trace the impact, both immediate and longterm, such laws had on poverty. Pinochet's regime led to what is now called the *feminization of poverty*. In every country surveyed thus far, the focus has been on poverty confronting women and children. So not surprisingly, poverty rates increased under Pinochet. By 1990, 40% of Chileans were living below the poverty line. Chile's decline in poverty since 1990 is comparable to Brazil's, but two issues stand out: income inequality still persists, so though women are forced into flexible and unstable jobs, they are paid less than men; the child poverty rate is

---

[48] Ibid. [47]

~22%.[49] These two issues are related to one another in such a way that the former causes the latter.

In Chile, the *feminization of poverty* resulted in more women entering the labor market. Due to this, there are a number of households where women are the head of household. Since 1990, there has "been a significant increase in the number of female heads of household, particularly amongst the poor, partly because of the break up of relationships, and partly because of men leaving to seek employment."[50] Given income inequality in women and the lack of an employed male in many households, children continue to be affected by poverty.

Despite a decrease in poverty overall, down to 14.4% in 2013[51], a 64% decrease over a period of just

---

[49] "SOS Children Villages in Chile". *SOS Children's Villages International*. ND. Web. 4 Dec 2018.

[50] Barrientos, Stephanie. "The other side of economic success: poverty, inequality, and women in Chile". Focus on Gender, 1(3): 38-40. 1993. Web. 4 Dec 2018. <https://pubmed.ncbi.nlm.nih.gov/12320730/>

[51] "Fewer Chileans living in poverty despite economic slowdown". *Reuters*. 22 Sep 2016. Web. 4 Dec 2018. <https://fr.reuters.com/article/uk-chile-poverty-idAFKCN11S2CD>

over two decades, child poverty remains high by comparison. This results in what should be an obvious observation: gender-driven income inequality results in high poverty rates in women and children. This is the case because the proverbial solution to household poverty is the woman being forced to earn an income. Some of those households, as is seen in Chile, come to be headed by women, so aside from eventually losing the income earned by their male counterparts, women are not able to improve their economic prospects. This highlights what should be a primary point of focus when discussing abortion: abortion is a quality-of-life issue that has heavier implications on the rights of women beyond *just* bodily autonomy. The insidious presence of poverty in the decision to have an abortion implies a gender-based income gap that is without an efficacious solution.

    Prior to surveying the role of domestic violence in the decision to have an abortion, it will be useful to cross the Atlantic, so to speak, and survey cases that will indubitably and unfortunately be markedly similar to the cases already explored. The focus will be on religious epicenters so that my more skeptical reader can see that religious belief does not hold much weight in the decision to have an abortion. Poverty is what features most prominently in the decision to have an abortion and this will be further proved in the Philippines and the Muslim World.

Poverty and Abortion in The Philippines: A Brief Overview

South America, generally speaking, yields a maternal mortality rate of about 10 times higher than that of Europe.[52] The rate in the Philippines is comparable and a cause for public concern. 610,000 women had abortions in 2012 and over 100,000 of them were hospitalized. Every day, three women die due to complications after undergoing unsafe procedures.[53] Padilla explains that roughly 90% of

---

[52] Ibid. [47]

[53] Padilla, Clara Rita. "The reality of abortion in the Philippines". *Rappler*. 13 Sep 2015. Web. 4 Dec 2018. <https://www.rappler.com/voices/ispeak/reality-abortion-philippines>

women who have abortions identify as Catholics. That should give my more skeptical readers pause. Religious belief does not deter women from getting abortions, so stricter laws based on religious precepts will not result in a widespread denunciation of abortion. The question to focus on is not so much how to deter women from making the decision to have an abortion, but rather, how can we improve their circumstances so that they are economically and emotionally ready to raise a child. We will no doubt return to this question, but for the time being, as has been done in each of the previous cases, the focus will be placed on poverty, especially in women and children.

For now, we must focus on just how dire the situation is in the Philippines. Imagine being outside of the site of the Black Nazarene, Quiapo Church, in the capital of the Philippines, Manila. The 400-year-old church, one of the most venerated religious centers in the Philippines, welcomes tens of thousands of pilgrims a year. Outside of the church, vendors sell alternative medicine, mainly in the forms of herbs and elixirs. There are on-site faith healers and fortune-tellers. In black sedans, there are vendors of another sort, vendors who sell a bitter herb to a woman who might be one of three women to die from post-abortion complications on any given day. As one of these herbalists, going by the codename, Elsa, explains, "these plants are very bitter — so bitter that the body can't take it. They'll make her blood come out. And the baby will come out with it."[54]

As Winn, writing for The Week, explains, this is what healthcare looks like for women in the Philippines seeking an abortion. A crime network of herbalists comprised of predominantly middle-aged women is too often the last resort for women with unwanted pregnancies. This is the case because legislators turn to the Vatican for moral and legal counsel. Because of this, there is no abortion debate in the Philippines. The debate is a settled matter and any woman who gets an abortion is a murderer liable

---

[54] Winn, Patrick. "In the Philippines, abortion is illegal. So desperate women are turning to elixirs.". *The Week.* 1 Sept 2017. Web. 31 Jan 2019. <https://theweek.com/articles/722003/philippines-abortion-illegal-desperate-women-are-turning-elixirs>

to serve six years in prison. As the Revised Penal Code of the Philippines outlines: "Any woman who shall commit this offense to conceal her dishonor, shall suffer the penalty of prison correctional in its minimum and medium periods."[55]

Apart from illegal herbs, there are other, more painful, abortion methods that women seek out. Women who want to end an unwanted pregnancy may get a hard stomach massage that is done daily for one week in hopes of inducing an abortion. This method is particularly painful and as abortion advocate, Marevic Parcon puts it, "torturous." To make it look like an accident, some women have thrown themselves down stairs. Others use hangers and barbecue sticks.[56] There are people on all sides of the abortion debate who scoff at the mention of

---

[55] Robles, Chan. "The Revised Penal Code of The Philippines". *Virtual Law Library*. ND. Web. 31 Jan 2019. <https://www.un.org/Depts/los/LEGISLATIONANDTREATIES/PDFFILES/PHL_revised_penal_code.pdf>

[56] Spera, Claudine. "How bitter herbs and botched abortions kill three women a day in the Philippines". *The Guardian*. 10 Jul 2017. Web. 31 Jan 2019.<https://www.theguardian.com/global-development/2017/jul/10/how-bitter-herbs-and-botched-abortions-kill-three-women-a-day-in-the-philippines>

hangers and underground clinics, but what many people consider stories intended to appeal to emotion are actually, in part, the harsh realities women in the Philippines are confronted with. There are harsher realities still as women have resorted to faking accidental falls and seeking out illegal herbalists.

Once again, these realities paint a much grimmer picture. Women in the Philippines are relegated to domestic roles that in parts of the West are considered outmoded or *traditional*. 84% of their time is allocated to childcare, for example. The ratio of poor women to poor children in the Philippines is nearly one-to-one as 11.2 million women are in poverty compared to 12.4 million children. Unlike Brazil and Chile, these trends have remained roughly stable due to the domestication of women. If women are not stay-at-home moms, they are confined to stereotypical employment opportunities, e.g., secretarial work, hospitality. This leaves them with little opportunity for economic upward mobility and when one adds that educational opportunities for women are just as limited, they are left with no escape from poverty.[57]

Given the fact that there is already precedence for helping women and children escape poverty, one might ask why do these trends persist in the Philippines, especially given that they have not persisted in countries like Brazil and Chile. Though what follows has been treated to a much greater extent, it has been suggested that the religious culture in the Philippines is to blame. Gender role attitudes that are informed by Catholic precepts have resulted in strata that categorize men and women, and therefore, give them distinct roles and rights. This facilitates the persistence of gender-based economic inequality.

One can go into exhaustive detail about the role religion plays in gender attitudes, but for current purposes, it is important to highlight that according to Edgell and Docka, the prevailing thought is that

---

[57] Rodriguez, Fritzie. "Why many of the hungry are women". *Rappler*. 25 Mar 2014. Web. 31 Jan 2019. <https://r3.rappler.com/move-ph/issues/hunger/53801-gender-inequality-women-hunger>

men develop in the public sphere while women develop in the private sphere. In other words, men are the proverbial breadwinners; women are to tend to the home and rear children.[58] Catholic attitudes in the Philippines and, arguably, elsewhere or arguably everywhere, reinforce patriarchal values and this stands to benefit men while putting women at an economic disadvantage.

At best, the government in the Philippines can be considered a quasi-theocratic regime. With regard to the country's laws prohibiting and criminalizing abortion, it has taken the Vatican's counsel too seriously. In other respects, the laws can reflect secular values and are not tied to Catholicism in any way. The Muslim World, on the other hand, is home to true theocratic regimes. So while there is still hope in the Philippines, especially given President Rodrigo Duerte's plan to reduce poverty, the situation in, especially the more religiously conservative parts of the Muslim World, is much bleaker. To this we now

---

[58] Edgell, P., & Docka, D. (2007). Beyond the nuclear family? Familism and gender ideology in diverse religious communities. *Sociological Forum, 22*(1), 25–50.

turn as it is necessary to demonstrate, especially to skeptical readers, that abortions are sought out despite religious beliefs and prohibitive abortion policies.

Poverty and Abortion in The Muslim World: A Brief Overview

Due to the pressure put on Muslim-majority countries to make their abortion policies more liberal, it would be a mistake to think of the Muslim World as a monolith.[59] The diverse abortion policies throughout the Muslim World convey an intricate history — one demonstrating what happens when a country transitions from restrictive abortion policies to more liberal ones. There are some countries that have succumbed to the pressure to liberalize their abortion policies while others have not liberalized their policies. Among the countries that have liberalized their policies, there are some that have

---

[59] Bowen DL. Brockopp JE. Contemporary Muslim ethics of abortion, *Islamic Ethics of Life: Abortion, War and Euthanasia* , 2003ColumbiaUniversity of South Carolina Press

problems with respect to the access women have to reproductive healthcare. In order to condense the history of abortion rights in the Muslim World, it will prove useful to discuss three countries in particular. Afghanistan has some of the most restrictive abortion policies in the Muslim World. Turkey has liberalized its abortion policies, but has continued to deal with the fact that many women in the country have no access to reproductive healthcare; also, Turkey currently faces political pressure to return to more prohibitive policies. Finally, Albania has liberalized its abortion laws, but its history can, in a sense, help to predict what will happen in Turkey now that Tayyip Erdogan is President.

      The situation in Afghanistan is not unlike what we have seen in Chile and in the Philippines. Abortion is illegal per Afghanistan's penal code. Any woman who is convicted of having an abortion and any person complicit in her abortion can serve up to seven years in prison or is required to pay a fine. Should a severe disability be identified in the fetus or if the woman's life is in mortal danger, exceptions are made. Rape and incest do not qualify as sufficient grounds for terminating a pregnancy.[60]

Of all the countries in Asia, Afghanistan has the highest birth rate. Afghan women have an average of six children and some may not want or would prefer to have fewer children. Many are simply not educated enough to know about contraception; nearly 80% of women in Afghanistan do not use birth control.[61] Furthermore, Afghanistan's infant mortality rate of 117.23 out of 1,000 live births is the highest in the world and its maternal mortality rate of 460 deaths for every 100,000 live births is the 22nd highest in the world. The mortality rates stem from

---

[60] Shapiro, Gilla. Abortion law in Muslim-majority countries: an overview of the Islamic discourse with policy implications, *Health Policy and Planning*, Volume 29, Issue 4, 1 July 2014, Pages 483–494, https://doi.org/10.1093/heapol/czt040

[61] Hasrat-Nazimi, Waslat. "Abortion in Afghanistan". *Qantara*. 5 May 2014. Web. 4 Feb 2019. <https://en.qantara.de/content/abortion-in-afghanistan-trying-to-break-a-major-societal-taboo>

the same sources: lack of access to healthcare and poverty.[62]

The lack of access to reproductive healthcare is no mystery in a country with prohibitive abortion policies. Women in Afghanistan either take pills that they acquire illegally in hopes of inducing an abortion or they turn to traditional midwives. Both methods are extremely risky as they can result in further complications, which often involve incessant bleeding.[63] Midwives seldom have the training and resources to address such complications. In Afghanistan, living in poverty can factor into a woman's decision to have an abortion. Islam also plays a large role and this is just another example of how gender role attitudes informed by religious precepts — in this case, Islamic precepts — facilitate gender-based economic inequality. Once again, one

---

[62] Reisler, Justine. "Infant and Maternal Mortality in Afghanistan". *NAOC*. 25 Jul 2014. Web. 4 Feb 2019. <http://natoassociation.ca/infant-and-maternal-mortality-in-afghanistan/>

[63] Ibid. [61]

can reasonably expect poverty rates to be highest for women.

Afghanistan ranks 169 out of 187 countries, with a gender inequality index of 0.705.[64] Briefly, the gender inequality index (GII) takes three factors into account: health, empowerment, and the labor market. Of these three factors, two of them account for two dimensions. For health, maternal mortality and adolescent birth rate, specifically the birth of every 1,000 women ages 15 to 19, are accounted for. For empowerment, the percentage of the population with secondary education and how many government seats are occupied by men and women are accounted for. The labor market measurement simply accounts for how many men versus how many women are employed.[65]

As mentioned earlier, Afghanistan's birth and maternal mortality rates are the highest in the world,

---

[64] Carter, Will. "Widowhood in Afghanistan". *Lacuna*. 2015 Jul 23. Web. 4 Feb 2019. <https://lacuna.org.uk/equality/widowhood-in-afghanistan/>

[65] Human Development Indices and Indicators: ... Statistical Update. , 2018. Web.<http://hdr.undp.org/sites/default/files/hdr2018_technical_notes.pdf>

and thus, contribute negatively to Afghanistan's GII. With respect to education, there have been improvements in childhood education. In 2001, boys comprised all of the roughly 900,000 children that attend school. As of 2016, girls made up 40% of the approximately nine million children that attend school. Though the literacy gap has also improved, boys are still ~53.5% more literate than girls.[66] This gap widens when the focus is secondary education. At the primary level, a 0.63 literacy gap increases to 0.48 in college and 0.38 in high school respectively. Girls not only enroll less in high school and college, but of the girls that do enroll, some attend classes infrequently while some do not attend at all.[67]

Because of a law enacted in 2004, Afghanistan's lower house parliament must reserve 25% of its seats to women. As of 2014, 28% of

---

[66] "Women and Girls in Afghanistan". *Razia's Ray of Hope Foundation*. ND. 9 Jul 2013. Web. <https://www.unwomen.org/en/news/stories/2013/7/afghani-women-strive-to-get-an-education>

[67] "Girls' Education in Afghanistan". *Oxfam*. 24 Feb 2011. Web. 4 Feb 2019. <https://www.oxfam.org/en/research/high-stakes-girls-education-afghanistan>

Afghanistan's parliamentary seats were held by women, a proportion that was then higher than the United States' 19%.[68] Many are opposed to this law, arguing that true equality is not achieved in this manner. Afghanistan is one of 40 countries with such a quota system in place.

This affirmative action-esque quota does not translate into labor force participation in general, which is 80% for males and 19% for women. Age factors very little into whether women are employed because they still face challenges, which include cultural attitudes with regard to the role of women, particularly in the household. As was observed in the Philippines, women are relegated to child-rearing and household chores. These prospects change dramatically for women with tertiary education; the unemployment rate for women with higher

---

[68] Crockett, Zachary. "Afghanistan Has More Women in National Parliament Seats Than the U.S.". *Priceonomics*. 30 Jan 2014. Web. 4 Feb 2019. <https://priceonomics.com/afghanistan-has-more-women-in-national-parliament/>

qualifications is just 3%.⁶⁹ The implication here is there is a class divide with respect to the employment opportunities women can access. More affluent women have better employment opportunities while women in poverty have fewer opportunities. This reveals a way forward for women in Afghanistan, which will no doubt be returned to later.

Living in poverty not only influences women in Afghanistan to seek abortions. It is also cited as one of the likelier reasons for why women commit suicide. Of the 1,800 Afghans who attempted suicide in 2017, about 1,400 were women.⁷⁰ If none of the other cases discussed painted a clear enough picture, Afghanistan certainly does. Poverty is often a precursor to the decision to have an abortion, but in turn, wherever abortion policies are restrictive and

---

⁶⁹ "Summary of The National Risk and Vulnerability Assessment 2007/8: A profile of Afghanistan". *Jehoon Printing Press*. ND. Web. 4 Feb 2019. <https://reliefweb.int/sites/reliefweb.int/files/resources/732AC034EAF0C654C125766500338844-Full_Report.pdf>

⁷⁰ Safi, Sana. "Why female suicide in Afghanistan is so prevalent". *BBC*. 1 Jul 2018. Web. 4 Feb 2019.<https://www.bbc.com/news/world-asia-44370711>

access to reproductive care limited, if not, almost entirely prohibited, women are forced to carry a pregnancy to term and end up raising, in Afghanistan's case, an average of six children. As has been shown, if women had more autonomy, they would certainly choose to have fewer children. It is time now to discuss another majority-Muslim country that is facing mounting political pressure to return to restrictive policies of old.

Though abortion has been legal in Turkey since 1983, access has always been a problem. Before discussing the current problem of access women in Turkey are confronted with, it is necessary to discuss the longstanding issue they were already dealing with. Despite the progress the country has made with respect to reproductive healthcare, women in some areas of the country could not access healthcare services. This was especially pronounced in rural areas and the impoverished eastern part of the country. Health facilities in rural areas often lack trained specialists, including gynecologists who are legally obligated to either perform or supervise abortions. Such facilities are thus excluded from providing these services.[71]

Access is absolutely crucial because the mortality rate in women who are forced to rely on unsafe abortion procedures is four times higher — 208 out of every 100,000 procedures compared with 49 out of every 100,000 procedures done by trained specialists.[72] Women in urban and more affluent areas of the country did not have to contend with this problem. However, an all-new problem threatens women across the country. Though Turkish President, Tayyip Erdogan, has not reversed the legalization of abortion, it is believed that he is behind a de facto ban on abortion that has made it much more difficult for women to get a safe, legal procedure. Public hospitals in 53 Turkish provinces reject abortion requests made solely by pregnant women. Abortions are prohibited in all hospitals in regions near the

---

[71] Igde, Fusun Artiran et al. "Abortion in Turkey: women in rural areas and the law" British journal of general practice : the journal of the Royal College of General Practitioners vol. 58,550 (2008): 370-3.<https://www.ncbi.nlm.nih.gov/pmc/articles/PMC2435661/>

[72] Ibid. [71]

Mediterranean and Black Seas. Of the country's 431 public hospitals, only 7.8% of them allow abortions that are requested by a pregnant woman and 11.8% refuse to perform abortions citing a matter of principle.[73]

Even for women who have access to safe procedures, the costs are often too high. In a country where one-third of women are employed and where the average household income is below American and European averages, 900 or more Turkish lire is beyond their reach. An abortion after the tenth week can cost upwards of 1,600 lire. Once one considers that the state does not cover the costs of an abortion requested by a pregnant woman, one quickly realizes that women face an uphill battle.[74] What is more unfortunate is that Erdogan's ban is far too many steps in the wrong direction. Albanian women have already been forced to go down a road paved by

---

[73] Karakas, Burcu. "Turkey's women face dangerous conditions to obtain legal abortion". *DW*. 27 Jan 2019. Web. 7 Feb 2019. <https://www.dw.com/en/turkeys-women-face-dangerous-conditions-to-obtain-legal-abortion/a-47257680>

[74] Ibid. [73]

prohibitive abortion policies; they have already grappled with the problem of access to reproductive healthcare.

Though it had been difficult to obtain accurate statistics on abortion prior to 1989, a recent study on the years between 1960 and 1980 was made available in October of 2017. During the two-decade period, the infant mortality rate was 86.3 for every 1,000 live births. There were over 209,000 registered abortions despite its illegality at the time; the number is thought to be much higher as many women turned to illegal procedures to avoid legal consequences.[75] Though this particular study does not provide statistics on the maternal mortality rate during that time, Sina and Teta estimate that between 1980 and 1990, 55% of maternal deaths were caused by illegal

---

[75] Mejdini, Fatjona. "Communist Albania Saw Increased Abortions, Infant Mortality". *Balkan Insight.* 27 Oct 2017. Web. 7 Feb 2019.<https://balkaninsight.com/2017/10/27/abortions-and-children-death-in-albania-show-plight-of-communism-10-27-2017/>

abortions or complications related to an illegal procedure.[76]

By 1991, abortion was legal and available upon request. By 1995, there were no instances where a woman died due to an illegal abortion. Infant mortality decreased by 65.2%, to 30 out of every 1,000 live births in 1995. By the year 2000, infant mortality decreased another 16.7%, from 30 to 25 out of every 1,000 live births. The year 2000 would have also marked the end of a bad turn for abortion policies as the government enacted a strict pro-birth policy in the interest of increasing the country's population by one million by that year. Fortunately, for women in Albania, the 90s saw a gradual end to the prohibitive abortion policies that flourished under Albanian Communism in the 80s.[77]

---

[76] Sina, Margalina and Teta, Olsian. "Albania: Legalisation Reduces Abortions And Maternal Deaths". 15 Aug 1996. Web. 7 Feb 2019. <http://www.ipsnews.net/1996/08/albania-legalisation-reduces-abortions-and-maternal-deaths/>

[77] "Women of the World: Laws and Policies Affecting Their Reproductive Lives: East Central Europe". *The Center for Reproductive Law and Policy*. Aug 2000. Web. 7 Feb 2019. <https://www.reproductiverights.org/sites/crr.civicactions.net/files/documents/TOCandIntro.pdf>

In this, Erdogan can learn a valuable lesson that will vastly reduce the negative impacts women in Turkey are currently facing. The return of restrictive policies also marks the return of illegal contraceptive and abortion methods, which, in turn, are a prelude to higher maternal deaths. Turkey, like Albania before it, must not go back to the days when abortion was criminalized. There is precedence in the Muslim World and in the world at large that should discourage Erdogan from continuing his de facto ban on abortion and eventually passing legislation that would officially ban abortion. If nothing else, the history of reproductive rights in the Muslim World not only serves as exemplary for majority-Muslim countries, but also countries around the world — especially countries currently enforcing prohibitive abortion policies.

Restrictive policies do not end abortion. Such policies end the lives of many women. In country after country, women literally bleed to death after experiencing complications related to unsafe, illegal procedures. Legalizing and decriminalizing abortion not only saves their lives, but also slows the cycle of poverty. For women in Afghanistan, the Philippines, Chile, Brazil, Northern Ireland, and other countries not surveyed here, the battle is ongoing. We are morally obligated to see what measures need to be taken in order to provide these women with safe, legal access to reproductive healthcare. Also, once this access is provided, we must ensure that there are no barriers keeping some women, be it for economic, educational, or other reasons, from getting and being able to meet the costs related to reproductive healthcare.

    We will return to these questions following the next chapter, but prior to that, it will prove crucial to discuss domestic violence and its relation to the decision to have an abortion. Domestic violence is often overlooked, but relationship and marital abuse often underly the decision to have an abortion. Therefore, apart from doing away with prohibitive policies and providing legal, safe reproductive care, we also have to ensure that a woman is *safe* in her own home.

2

Notable Statistical Trends on Abortion: Domestic Violence and Related Issues

Because the data on domestic violence and abortion are scarcer in comparison to the data discussed in the previous chapter, fewer cases will be discussed. The United States, Northern Ireland, and England will be revisited, since researchers in the US and the UK have done plenty of work on the link between domestic violence and abortion. Then a new country will be surveyed, namely Australia, as researchers there have made progress to make the link between domestic violence and abortion clearer. Primarily, a few general facts have to be kept in mind.

Women who have experienced domestic violence have poorer reproductive health when compared to women who have not experienced abuse.[78] Domestic violence has also been linked to

---

[78] Coker, A.L. (2007). Does physical intimate partner violence affect sexual health? A systematic review. *Trauma, Violence & Abuse*, 8(2), 149-177.

unwanted pregnancy, repeat abortions, and miscarriages.[79] Women who have abusive partners are often prevented from using contraception and are also victims of date rape. Both of these factors result in an unwanted pregnancy.[80] It is also crucial to bear in mind that domestic violence is not limited to physical forms of abuse and that what Moore, Frohwirth, and Miller coined as "reproductive control" includes economic and emotional components.[81]

The economic component may involve a woman's abusive partner refusing to give her money to purchase contraception or to get an abortion. The abusive partner might also deny paternity or accuse her of cheating, both serving as forms of emotional

---

[79] Williams, C.M., Larsen, U., & McCloskey, L.A. (2008). Intimate partner violence and women's contraceptive use. *Violence Against Women,* 14(12), 1382-1396.

[80] Lathrop, A. (1998). Pregnancy resulting from rape. Journal of Obstetrics, Gynecologic and Neonatal Nursing, 1998, 27(1), 25-31.

[81] Moore, A.M., Frohwirth, L., Miller, E. (2010). Male reproductive control of women who have experienced intimate partner violence in the United States. *Social Science and Medicine,* 70 (11), 1737-1744.

abuse.[82] Moore, Frohwirth, and Miller do not mention forms of verbal abuse, which include various ways of making her feel insecure such as making negative remarks about her weight or some other aspect of her appearance that she is already insecure about, and/or degrading her with profane name-calling and insults. Verbal forms of abuse also constitute emotional abuse because a woman's self-esteem inevitably decreases. Verbal and emotional forms of abuse are perhaps better captured by the term *psychological abuse*. It is time now to revisit the United States for purposes of better establishing a link between domestic abuse and abortion.

Domestic Violence and Abortion in the United States: A Brief Overview

Evins and Chescheir, in one of the earlier studies linking domestic violence and abortion, reported that 7.8% of women seeking an abortion at an American university clinic disclosed current

---

[82] Ibid. [81]

instances of domestic violence in their relationships while 21.6% disclosed abuse within the prior year.[83] Of a sample size of 486 women, 39.5% of them had a history of domestic violence and difficulties in their relationships were the sole reason given as to why they were looking to terminate their pregnancies.[84] To put this into perspective, 192 women were looking to terminate their pregnancies solely due to the fact that they had suffered domestic abuse.

Unfortunately, the situation has not changed. What is more unfortunate still is that women who experience abuse may be caught between the proverbial rock and hard place. In some cases, a woman experiences abuse because she terminated her pregnancy while in others, she experiences abuse because her partner wants to force her to continue an unwanted pregnancy. Having an abortion could result in a decrease in physical violence while also making it

---

[83] Evins G, Chescheir N. Prevalence of domestic violence among women seeking abortion services. *Women's Health Issues* 1996;6:204–10. doi:10.1016/1049-3867(95)00012-7

[84] Glander S, Moore M, Michielutte R, Parsons L. The prevalence of domestic violence among women seeking abortion. *Obstet Gynecol* 1998;91:1002–6. doi:10.1016/S0029-7844(98)00089-1

easier for a woman to leave an abusive partner. On the other hand, carrying an unwanted pregnancy to term often results in continued violence and makes it much harder for a woman to leave an abusive relationship. Women who choose to stay with an abusive partner post-abortion are likely to experience sustained abuse.[85]

What is often overlooked is that a woman might have already had a child with an abusive partner. Children in abusive relationships are often abused as well. In the United States, conservative-leaning states that have adopted restrictive policies are exposing women and children to ongoing abuse.[86] Given the results of the study, looser policies should be adopted so that women feel no obligation to stay in an abusive relationship and so that they retain autonomy and final say over whether or not they continue their pregnancies. In light of the studies in the United States hitherto discussed, one can

---

[85] Roberts et al. (2014) Risk of violence from the man involved in the pregnancy after receiving or being denied an abortion. *BMC Medicine*. 12:144

[86] Ibid. [85]

conclude that domestic violence goes beyond the decision to have an abortion and extends much further into any discussion on women's rights. The decision to have a child is one of the larger decisions a couple can make, so if an abusive partner can assume full control over that decision, one can infer that he has assumed control over most other decisions. State governments should be doing everything in their power to help women avoid staying in abusive relationships.

Domestic Violence and Abortion in the UK: A Brief Overview

Domestic violence probably factored in Northern Ireland's recent reversal of its longstanding abortion ban. Briefly, at the outset of this work, Northern Ireland retained some of the more prohibitive policies in Europe. The country is a great example of the fluid, changing landscape of abortion policies around the world. Since the reversal of these policies warrants a closer look, that will be discussed in the next chapter. For now, the persistent connection between abortion and domestic violence during the country's ban on abortion will come into focus.

One of the more alarming examples of domestic violence is reproductive control. Maya Oppenheim, writing for The Independent, shared the accounts of Dawn Purvis, former director of the Marie Stopes pregnancy advice service in Belfast. While one of these accounts is particularly graphic, the testimonial shows the severity of reproductive control:

She had a contraceptive implant so he sat on her chest and cut out the implant with a stanley knife. That is why she had her arm wrapped up. He had raped her and had been raping her for weeks after that. Her face was a punch bag and she was in floods of tears saying 'I can't have a child with this man. He will kill me and he will kill my son. I know that. I have to get away now'.[87]

---

[87] Oppenheim, Maya. "Northern Ireland's abortion ban: The harrowing experiences of domestic violence survivors and underage girls looking for help". *The Independent*. 3 Feb 2019. Web. <https://www.independent.co.uk/news/uk/home-news/northern-ireland-abortion-ban-domestic-violence-underage-marie-stopes-dawn-purvis-a8758711.html>

Violent forms of reproductive control tend to be common when the would-be father does not want his partner to continue the pregnancy. One particular case in London also highlights the consequences that are confronting women who have illegal abortions. Harief Pearson, his cousin, Kydie McKenna, and an unnamed 16-year-old girl kidnapped and repeatedly assaulted a 17-year-old girl Pearson impregnated. Their intention was to cause a miscarriage because Pearson did not want to be a father.[88] The 16-year-old assailant made the victim drink detergent, so that the victim would face jail-time in the event of a miscarriage.[89] Had the assailants escaped justice, the victim would have faced jail-time for allegedly causing herself to have a miscarriage.

---

[88] Duggan, Richard. "Thugs forced a pregnant teenager to drink detergent so she would suffer a miscarriage". *MyLondon*. 11 Jun 2019. Web. <https://www.mylondon.news/news/west-london-news/thugs-forced-pregnant-teenager-drink-16411324>

[89] Hockaday, James. "Trio jailed for pouring detergent down pregnant teen's throat to force an abortion". *Metro UK*. 8 Jul 2019. Web. <https://metro.co.uk/2019/07/08/trio-jailed-pouring-detergent-pregnant-teens-throat-force-abortion-10135068/>

The Domestic Abuse Bill will be discussed further in the next chapter because the bill once again makes clear the connection between domestic violence and abortion. A connection had already been made in a 2012 cross-sectional study that noted that domestic violence is more frequent during pregnancy. Given this, whether domestic violence factors into a woman's decision to terminate her pregnancy is a pertinent question. The study found that instances of domestic abuse fluctuate between 7.8% during the pregnancy to anywhere between 12 and 22% the following year. The study also makes reference to two other studies showing that one-third of women have experienced lifetime domestic violence were six times likelier to suffer domestic violence during pregnancy.[90]

The link between the decision to terminate pregnancy and ongoing domestic violence is not merely tentative. This highlights the importance of

---

[90] Motta S, Penn-Kekana L, Bewley S Domestic violence in a UK abortion clinic: anonymous cross-sectional prevalence survey Journal of Family Planning and Reproductive Health Care 2015;41:128-133.

the Domestic Abuse Bill and the urgency lawmakers should have with respect to passing it. That domestic abuse can force a woman to either become pregnant or terminate pregnancy demonstrates that the connection persists. Prior to discussing ways in which this link can be severed, it is imperative to briefly examine the connection between domestic violence and abortion in Australia.

Domestic Violence and Abortion in Australia: A Brief Overview

As was observed in the UK, women in Australia have been coerced into pregnancy. Notably, the legality of abortion differed throughout Australia before 2019. Queensland, for instance, adhered to the NSW Crimes Act of 1900, which criminalized abortion. Rape, incest, and fetal disability were not sufficient grounds to terminate pregnancy, according to the act. A physician going by the pseudonym, Karen, stated: "A woman may have a partner who becomes violent and becomes very possessive, and a way of expressing ownership over that woman is forced pregnancy." She adds: "Women might not have access to funds because of the relationship, or they might have access to funds but they need to have an abortion discreetly because when their partner finds out then the relationship actually gets more violent."[91]

Domestic violence, to reiterate, is not merely physical. Male partners can also withhold financial resources as a means to control women—making it virtually impossible for them to afford contraceptives or abortion procedures, even in the parts of Australia where abortion was already legal. Children by Choice senior counselor Liz Price states: "You're much more physically vulnerable, you're much more economically dependent, your time outside of the home is much more restricted so it's much easier to hold a woman in place where other forms of violence

---

[91] Uibu, Katri. "Abortion laws making it harder for women to escape domestic violence, expert warns". *ABC AU*. 20 Jun 2017. Web. <https://www.abc.net.au/news/2017-06-21/abortion-laws-force-abused-women-to-stay-with-perpetrators/8451772>

and control can continue."[92] Price also alludes to a study showing a disturbing link between reproductive coercion and poor mental health. 36.6% of women who reported reproductive coercion exhibited mental health issues compared to 14.1% of women who did not report such coercion. The study assessed 3,117 women in Australia and also found that 17.8% of the women reported reproductive coercion in subsequent contact with their counselors. Only 5.9% reported it initially, which may suggest a reluctance to disclose the abuse they are dealing with.[93] This also suggests that domestic violence may play a much larger role in a woman's decision to have an abortion.

As in the UK, Australian lawmakers have been confronted by public demands for abortion reform. CEO of Rape and Domestic Violence Services

---

[92] Stevenson, Ashleigh. "Reproductive coercion affects one in three female domestic violence victims, study shows". *ABC AU*. 23 Jun 2019. Web. <https://www.abc.net.au/news/2019-06-24/reproductive-coercion-affecting-domestic-violence-survivors/11223778>

[93] Price, Elizabeth, et al. "Experiences of Reproductive Coercion in Queensland Women." *Journal of Interpersonal Violence*, May 2019, doi:10.1177/0886260519846851.

Australia, Karen Willis stated: "Keeping abortion in the Crimes Act ensures that it is women experiencing domestic or sexual violence that are the most disadvantaged. Refusing to address the health concerns of women in their time of need is cruel and puts their health in jeopardy." As of late 2019, abortion is now legal in every Australian state. It is allowable thru week 16 in Tasmania and thru week 28 in South Australia. On average, however, it is allowable thru weeks 22 and 24 — weeks extremely pivotal in determining fetal liability as will be shown later.[94]

    When considering the facts discussed in the previous and current chapters, it is imperative to discuss what can be done. Brazil's response to poverty, for instance, has been exemplary; responses to domestic violence in liberal-leaning states in the U.S. also pave the way for parts of the world that retain restrictive abortion policies. What can be done will consist, in large part, of what has already been

---

[94] Willis, Olivia. "Is abortion legal in Australia? It's complicated". *ABC News*. 25 May 2018. Web. <https://www.abc.net.au/news/health/2018-05-26/is-abortion-legal-in-australia/9795188>

done: legalizing abortion, so that procedures are safe; decriminalizing abortion, so that women have the choice to terminate pregnancy without having to worry about facing jail-time; protecting women from domestic violence, so that they are free to disclose abuse; lifting women out of poverty by way of educational and employment opportunities. Northern Ireland's reversal of restrictive abortion policies will be revisited, for it is a development that unfolded during this work. The interest there will be in the changes one can reasonably expect, specifically as it concerns mortality and poverty rates, abortion rates per capita, and so on. As of right now, it is too soon to tell what kind of impact legalization of abortion will have, so what is left is an extrapolation from the data of countries that have implemented similar changes to their laws.

3
What Can Be Done

As previously stated, what can be done is already mirrored, in part, in what has been done. For instance, in the United States, after the Roe v. Wade decision in 1973, abortion was decriminalized and legalized. Liberal-leaning states have also enacted injunctions against domestic violence and by extension, reproductive coercion. Employment opportunities have also been made available to women living in poverty. The same can be said of Brazil, with respect to its success in reducing poverty, and the states in Australia that have legalized abortion. We will revisit some of the regions previously discussed in order to arrive at a consensus with respect to what countries with restrictive policies should do to lift women and children out of poverty and lower mortality rates.; also of interest will be arriving at a consensus concerning further steps to be taken in countries that have legalized and decriminalized abortion because as will be demonstrated shortly, such countries can do more to improve sex education and education more generally, alleviate poverty, reduce infant and maternal mortality rates, and deter domestic violence. It is time now to revisit Northern Ireland to survey important changes to their abortion policies and to predict the net impact these changes will eventually have.

At the outset of this project, Northern Ireland adhered to one of the most restrictive policies in the world. Northern Ireland operated under the 1861 Offenses Against the Person Act, which prohibited abortion. That act was coupled with the 1945 Criminal Justice Act, which criminalized abortion and carried a potential life sentence. After a week of mounting legal pressure, Northern Ireland's Department of Health authorized abortion services on April 9th of 2020, enforcing legislation that overturned the region's restrictive policies.

Specifically, the Creasy amendment resulted in the repeal of sections 58 and 59 of the Offenses Against the Person Act. Any prosecutions still in order were dismissed and for a short period, the UK government funded travel for residents of Northern Ireland seeking abortion services in England. Abortion in Northern Ireland is now legal through the first 12 weeks of pregnancy.[95] While it is still too soon to trace the positive effects the Creasy Amendment will have, necessary extrapolations can be made via scrutiny of similar changes in other regions. For such purposes, it will prove crucial to revisit the United States.

In 1965, illegal abortions comprised one-sixth of all pregnancy-related deaths according to official reports. The actual total may be much higher. Restrictive abortion policies, as was shown to be the case in the regions discussed, harmed low-income families the most. In the 1960s, one survey conducted among low-income women in New York City who terminated their pregnancies found that 80% of them attempted to self-induce; illegal abortion accounted

---

[95] Sheldon, S., O'Neill, J., Parker, C. and Davis, G. (2020), 'Too Much, too Indigestible, too Fast'? The Decades of Struggle for Abortion Law Reform in Northern Ireland. The Modern Law Review, 83: 761-796. doi:10.1111/1468-2230.12521

for one-sixth of pregnancy-related deaths in 1965.[96] Fast forward to today and one finds that abortion-related deaths are statistically rare, three in every one million abortions at eight weeks gestation.[97]

In August of 2020, New York State Governor Andrew Cuomo signed into law three bills "allowing domestic violence victims to file a complaint to any agency statewide"; this will ensure that "individuals will be provided with the ability to report crimes without fear or intimidation by their abuser." Domestic violence victims who leave the state or even the country are also able to vote by way of an absentee ballot.[98] It is vital to provide domestic violence victims a way of reporting abuse and it is

---

[96] NA. "Roe v. Wade: The Constitutional Right to Access Safe, Legal Abortion". *Planned Parenthood*. ND. Web. <https://www.plannedparenthoodaction.org/issues/abortion/roe-v-wade>

[97] Zane, Suzanne et al. "Abortion-Related Mortality in the United States: 1998-2010." *Obstetrics and gynecology* vol. 126,2 (2015): 258-65. doi:10.1097/AOG.0000000000000945

[98] Arnold, Chad. "Domestic violence in New York: How these new laws will help to protect victims". *Democrat & Chronicle*. 9 Aug 2019. Web. <https://www.democratandchronicle.com/story/news/politics/albany/2019/08/09/domestic-abuse-victims-getting-these-new-protections-ny/1965582001/>

just as crucial to protecting victims after they have reported abuse. Despite New York's success with respect to domestic violence, it takes part in the country's abject failure to reduce poverty and ensure that children and young adults receive adequate sex education.

    Prior to focusing attention on education, there is a dimension concerning domestic violence that is not often discussed. It was mentioned earlier that there may be an issue with overall male psychology and that because of this, therapeutic measures should be taken to address abusive tendencies in males. People often err when they link domestic violence with an incapacity to manage anger. While anger always serves as a secondary emotion for more vulnerable emotions like frustration and disappointment, the need for an abuser to take control in a relationship and exert dominance over their partner is not reducible to an issue with anger management. Domestic violence stems from a desire to control and obtain power in a relationship. There is a sense of entitlement on the part of the abuser that drives him to seek power and control. This often results in ignoring his partner's emotions. The feelings that are being masked in abusive behaviors are inadequacy, guilt, low self-esteem, jealousy, or fear of abandonment.[99]

It follows then that preventative and intervention efforts have to be taken as soon as abusive tendencies come to light. The issue here is that given the private nature of most relationships, a third party is often not privy to any abuse in a couple. This would leave matters of prevention or intervention in the hands of the abuse victim. This is why it is crucial to stress the importance of normalizing domestic abuse hotlines and professionals that can be reached at any time, so that a victim does not feel as though she is getting her partner into legal trouble. If underlying feelings of inadequacy, guilt, and jealousy are present, the individual requires therapy; the couple might even benefit from regular therapy sessions, so that they

---

[99] Mitchel, Susan. "Is Domestic Violence an Anger Management Problem?". *Ascendant Behavioral Health*. ND. Web. <https://ascendantclinics.com/domestic-violence/>

can improve communication and have a safe space to share vulnerable feelings with one another.[100] The issue might be that the male in question has unresolved feelings about the abuse that he suffered from an abusive parent or guardian or from another source, like bullies at school; studies show that one-third of people who have experienced abuse eventually perpetrate abuse.[101]

Nordic countries have taken crucial steps into understanding the paradox of domestic abuse in a region that exhibits more parity between men and women. Steps have been taken to build a profile of abuse perpetrators in the region and rehabilitation has been offered to them. The difficulties therapists confront in these men are common in patients who exhibit destructive behavioral patterns, e.g., anger

---

[100] NA. "What to Expect in Couples Therapy: What Actually Happens in Couples Counseling?". *Our Relationship*. ND. Web. <https://www.ourrelationship.com/what-to-expect-in-couples-therapy-what-actually-happens-in-couples-counseling-2/>

[101] Madeleine, Holden. "Why Do Some Victims of Abuse Become Abusers Themselves — And Others Don't?". ND. Web. <https://melmagazine.com/en-us/story/why-victims-abuse-become-abusers>

management, drug and alcohol abuse. Abuse perpetrators in Nordic countries redefine the violence toward their partners by making it sound as though their partners did things to provoke them. Some of them go as far as making it sound like a fistfight; others accuse their partners of abusive behavior that prompted them to respond in like manner. More commonly, these men engage in dissociation by attempting to differentiate themselves from perpetrators they imagine are better examples of abusers. That is to say that while 25-30% of the perpetrators admit to having violent tendencies, they do not see themselves as domestic abusers.[102] Ultimately, this aspect of domestic violence should not be overlooked going forward, since improving the quality of life for families invariably involves improving the quality of life for the male partner in a relationship. The steps that are being taken in Nordic countries should be followed in any nation dealing

---

[102] Wemrell, M, Stjernlöf, S, Aenishänslin, J, Lila, M, Gracia, E, Ivert, A-K. Towards understanding the Nordic paradox: A review of qualitative interview studies on intimate partner violence against women (IPVAW) in Sweden. *Sociology Compass.* 2019; 13:e12699. https://doi.org/10.1111/soc4.12699

with the issue of domestic violence. It is time now to discuss how education can help mitigate the issues surrounding the decision to have an abortion.

    A primary concern is the lack of adequate sex education in the United States. New York City, for example, mandates sex education in middle schools and high schools. The State of New York, however, does not require sex education. As a result of this, students in public schools are given inaccurate information. Helen Wajda, writing for New York University, states the following: "A recent report by the New York Civil Liberties Union found that almost 2 in 3 school districts did not mention female genitalia, 1 in 3 did not teach students how to use condoms, and many did not even mention LGBTQ+ relationships or identities."[103] Wajda also mentions that sex education is required in 29 states, which means that 21 states do not require sex education. 19 of those states teach students that sex is only acceptable after marriage and all of the states tend to

---

[103] Wajda, Helen. "The Inadequacy of Sex Ed". *Washington Square News*. 24 Feb 2020. Web. <https://nyunews.com/opinion/2020/02/24/sex-education-new-york/>

stress abstinence.[104] This implies that the use of contraceptives and education with respect to abortion is largely absent in public classrooms across the United States.

Prior to elaborating on what accurate sex education should look like and sharing examples of the kind of curriculum that would be better suited to address the issues being discussed, it is important to stress the link poor education has to poverty. The poverty rate among girls and women in New York City is 17.9%. In low-income areas, more than 50% of women do not have a high school diploma. Going back to the fact that infant mortality rates are higher among poor women and lower among affluent women, the infant mortality rate among Black women in New York City is 8.6 deaths per every 1,000 births compared to 2.8 per 1,000 births among White women. Maternal mortality rates are also higher among Black women; 79 deaths per every 100,000 births while the mortality rate among White women

---

[104] Ibid.

is .01%.[105] The strong implication in these figures is that poor education in lower-income communities precipitates income inequality; that inequality is then inherent in infant and maternal mortality rates, as well as poverty rates across the city.

The question of how to best approach the issues of sex literacy, income inequality, and poverty requires a better solution than the ones employed in the United States. Despite having made abortion legal in 1973, that has not proven sufficient because conservative-leaning states continue to enforce restrictions and provide inadequate sex education. Mississippi, for instance, has not decriminalized abortion. Though the law is neither enforceable nor constitutional, having an abortion is punishable by up to ten years in prison. This applies to both the woman who terminates her pregnancy and the individual who provides abortion services. Providers can also have their licenses restricted or revoked, or can face

---

[105] Mason, Nicole C. "New York Women's Foundation Report". *The New York Women's Foundation.* Mar 2013. Web. <https://www.nywf.org/wp-content/uploads/2017/02/New-York-Womens-Foundation-Report.pdf>

suspension if they provide abortion services after 15 weeks.[106] Mississippi's laws closely resemble the laws of conservative-leaning states in the southern United States. Utah also criminalizes abortion and enforces strict policies.[107] So while lawmakers in New York have enacted injunctions against domestic violence, the vast majority of states across the country continue to fail women in poverty by not providing accurate sex education and even going as far as criminalizing and restricting abortion.

The fact of the matter is that many countries have failed to implement a solution that is exactly right. Brazil's response to poverty proves exemplary, but the country has not done enough on other fronts. Brazil's poverty rate has steadily decreased since 1980. The educational system in Brazil underwent a series of educational reforms since the

---

[106] ND. "State Laws: Mississippi". *Pro-Choice America*. ND. Web. <https://www.prochoiceamerica.org/state-law/mississippi/>

[107] ND. "Utah passes new abortion rules, could mean felony charges for doctors and women". *NBC News*. 13 Mar 2020. Web. <https://www.nbcnews.com/politics/politics-news/utah-passes-new-abortion-rules-could-mean-felony-charges-doctors-n1157881>

implementation of its new constitution in 1988. More emphasis was placed on primary and secondary education that was funded by the government. Public spending on education increased to as high as 4.5% of Brazil's GDP in the mid-1990s from 2.7% in 1980. School attendance for children between 7 and 14 years old was universalized in the 1990s.

Investments in post-secondary education were less biased and there was also an increase in public investment in education per student. The real public investment per student increased by 94% between 2000 and 2009, according to data from the Ministry of Education. Attendance rates also increased among teenagers between 15 and 17. This translated to a more educated workforce, with literacy rates dropping to 1.9% in people aged 15 to 24. The percentage of those who are employed or actively looking for jobs doubled in 15 years from about one-third of the country's population in 1980. Workers who obtained higher education also increased in that period. Brazil succeeded in helping its population become more educated while also ensuring that educational opportunities were distributed more fairly. This has decreased workforce inequality over a 15-year period and has also contributed significantly to the overall decrease in income inequality.[108]

Much more can be said about Brazil's anti-poverty policies and the country's failure to aide its population of Afro-Brazilians. As was the case with Blacks and Whites in the United States, there is a stark disparity between the incomes of White and Black Brazilians. Unemployment rates for Black Brazilians are 35% higher than that of Whites and the poverty rate was 33% among Black Brazilians and 14% for Whites as of 2007.[109][110] It should be clear

---

[108] Ferreira de Souza, Pedro H.G. "Poverty, Inequality and Social Policies in Brazil, *1995-2009*". *International Policy Centre for Economic Growth*. Feb 2012. Web. <https://www.econstor.eu/obitstream/10419/71804/1/687787998.pdf>

[109] Pereira, Claudiney. "Ethno-racial Poverty and Income Inequality in Brazil". *Commitment to Equity*. Nov 2016. Web. <https://www.commitmentoequity.org/publications_files/Brazil/CEQ_WP60_Pereira_Nov23_2016.pdf>

[110] Gradin, Carlos. "Why Is Poverty So High Among Afro-Brazilians?A Decomposition Analysis of the Racial Poverty Gap". *Universidade de Vigo and IZA*. May 2007. Web. <http://ftp.iza.org/dp2809.pdf>

that alleviating poverty in less homogeneous regions requires a level of inclusivity not seen in the United States or Brazil. This is an area where more diverse countries can improve.

Another area of interest is the implementation of a universal basic income, which Brazil implemented in response to the COVID-19 outbreak. The social program granted 600 reais to 30% of its population; the program extended to 50% of the population in June and in that same month, Brazil's poverty rate was just 3.3%.[111] The question will always be asked how long can any government sustain a welfare program of this sort. The answer depends on the wealth of the country in question, but rather than concentrate that wealth into the hands of the few, as was the case in nineteenth-century England when Marx observed the abuses proletariats endured under the bourgeoisie and as is the case in the United States where billionaires have seen their

---

[111] Lima, Sergio Mario, et. al. "Brazil Hands Out So Much Covid Cash That Poverty Nears a Low". *Bloomberg*. 2 Sep 2020. Web. <https://www.bloomberg.com/news/articles/2020-09-02/brazil-hands-out-so-much-covid-cash-that-poverty-nears-a-new-low>

wealth increase by $845 billion since the onset of the COVID-19 outbreak in March of 2020, wealth could be more fairly distributed by implementing a universal basic income — especially for families falling below the poverty line. A universal basic income will also alleviate poverty in marginalized racial groups and start to close the gap of income inequality among men and women and Whites and non-Whites in heterogeneous regions. Brazil, to its credit, has made great strides to combat poverty, but like other diverse regions, it has largely ignored ostracized ethnic groups. The Brazilian government has also harmed its prospects with respect to reducing poverty in women due to its adoption of restrictive abortion policies.

While many countries have not implemented a decisive strategy, Nordic countries have proven exemplary. In 2017, there were 74,000 induced abortions across Finland, Denmark, Norway, Sweden, and Iceland.[112] The total population of all Nordic

---

[112] NA. "Finland has the fewest induced abortions in the Nordic region". *Finnish Institute for Health and* Welfare. 25 Mar 2019. Web. <https://thl.fi/en/web/thlfi-en/-/finland-has-the-fewest-induced-abortions-in-the-nordic-region>

nations in 2017 was 27 million. Induced abortions therefore occurred at a rate of .27%. Abortion in the Nordic region is an extremely rare occurrence. This should no doubt make any pro-lifer happy, but for this to be the case globally, there is work to be done; strategies to reduce abortion rates have to be implemented.

    Brazil's response to poverty, the response to domestic violence on behalf of liberal-leaning states in the United States, Australia and Northern Ireland's reversals of restrictive abortion policies, and improved general and sex education have to be synthesized. Education is the most crucial step in alleviating the problem of abortion and since poor sex education has already been observed, the improvements that can be made are in plain view. Sex education in the United States focuses on abstinence and on the immorality of sex before marriage. It does not include much in the way of condom use, other contraceptives (e.g., IUD, Plan B, birth control pills), and the abortion services available to women looking to terminate an unwanted pregnancy.

It is therefore incumbent on any country looking to improve sex education to teach students the various ways pregnancy can be avoided. Abstinence is a way to avoid pregnancy, but it is unrealistic to expect all youth to abstain from having sex. Also, the outmoded method of teaching students about sexually transmitted infections and diseases for purposes of imposing fear in them is unacceptable. Students should learn about STDs, but only for sake of knowing why safe sex is important. Such lessons can occur in conjunction with lessons about condom use and it is imperative to teach students about other forms of contraceptives as well.

Veronica Honkasalo opposes the universalization of sex education, which has become a pressing issue. In heterogeneous countries, a universal curriculum simply has not worked. Honkasalo, for example, discusses the widespread issues students have with Finland's sex education classes. She explains:

The sex education provided by the schools did not get high marks from the young interviewees; instead, they emphasized that they gathered the best information about sexuality from popular culture, the media and their friends. The education provided by the schools was seen as old-fashioned and concentrating too much on anatomical and medical issues, even though the young people saw these subjects as being an elementary level for learning things. Many of the young people thought that the lessons on sexuality were embarrassing and ridiculous, even if the teacher had good intentions.[113]

Honkasalo goes on to explain that the curriculum excludes the taboos and norms of different cultures. One Muslim student, for instance, felt singled out when a teacher told her she did not have to watch a video of a woman giving birth if she did not want to. A Vietnamese student commented on the dating norms of her generation versus that of her parents' generation. Another student complained that more complicated questions do not receive sufficient reply. I agree with Honkasalo that "official

---

[113] Honkasalo, V. (2014). Exceptionalism and sexualism in Finnish sex education. *Global Studies of Childhood, 4*(4), 286–297. <https://journals.sagepub.com/doi/pdf/10.2304/gsch.2014.4.4.286>

sex education curriculum and the professional narratives that the educators produce cannot be seen in the framework of pure reason, but more attention should be paid to how these assumptions include religious, cultural and ideological notions of sexuality."[114]

    Moreover, sex educators need to be mindful of religious and cultural idiosyncrasies, systemic inequality, pleasure and desire, and homosexual and non-monogamist relationships. The classroom must also conduct itself more democratically, so that the experiences and questions students have are given ample attention. This would require sociologists and anthropologists to conduct research with respect to the interactions between students and teachers in a sex education classroom. The curriculum that develops from this project can then be employed on a global scale across any and all heterogeneous societies. The United States, for instance, would benefit greatly from a new curriculum since the current one is Christian-centric and excludes the

---

[114] Ibid.

cultural and religious norms of many of the country's citizens. Education, in general, should be drastically improved as observed in Brazil.

Though it may take several years to a decade to see a notable improvement in Northern Ireland, one can conclude, on the basis of what has been observed in countries that have legalized abortion, that circumstances will improve across the board in Northern Ireland. Northern Ireland might also do better than the United States, for instance, if it implemented broader, more inclusive sex education and consistent laws that aim to deter domestic violence. Northern Ireland can also succeed where the United States has failed with respect to attending to impoverished families, so that poverty rates improve in the future, especially among women and children. One area where drastic improvement can be expected is in pregnancy-related deaths that are due to illegal abortions. Also, low-income women travel will no longer have to travel to England to access abortion services.

I want to emphasize a specific area of education that is often overlooked. Brazil drastically lowered its poverty rate by implementing a universal basic income since the start of the COVID-19 pandemic. The question that needs to be stressed is how can one ensure that people formerly below the poverty line remain above it. In other words, one should endeavor to teach people who have been brought out of poverty to better manage their finances. Financial literacy is vital, most especially among marginalized ethnic groups.

The issue, similar to the problem with current sex education curriculums, is that financial literacy curriculums cannot be universalized. Financial literacy classes also have to be mindful of religious and cultural norms. As Sandra Huston contends:

Some research suggests that financial education does not have a significant effect on improving financial knowledge scores of high school students in the United States contends that the costs of financial education programs outweigh potential benefits. In contrast, other studies support a relationship between financial education, financial literacy and positive financial outcomes. These mixed results may indicate that not all financial education programs are equally effective, that factors other than financial literacy contribute to financial distress or both.[115]

Among those factors may be the fact that a student might be the child of working-class parents. If she has grown accustomed to her family living paycheck to paycheck, then she is under specific financial distress that differs markedly from the experience of a student in a middle-class family. A middle-class student's parents, in contrast, can withdraw money from their retirement savings or from their investment accounts. They have high credit scores and can therefore extend their lines of credit. His family is then more capable of meeting a pressing financial need. The student from the working-class family, on the other hand, has experiences that are decidedly different from those of the middle-class student. Financial literacy educators

---

[115] Huston, S.J. (2010), Measuring Financial Literacy. Journal of Consumer Affairs, 44: 296-316. doi:10.1111/j.1745-6606.2010.01170.x

would therefore have to be mindful of an array of circumstances their students may be experiencing.

It would be incumbent on researchers to closely examine the interactions of instructors and students, so that financial literacy curriculums can be improved. The simplest approach, especially among wealthier nations, would be to distribute wealth more fairly, so that the financial distress experienced by working-class families becomes a thing of the past. The truth of the matter is that working-class citizens cannot make much use of financial literacy know-how. They can acquire knowledge, but without the necessary financial resources, they cannot apply that knowledge. When a parent works to make ends meet, there is often enough to pay bills and meet their needs, but very little disposable income and they are therefore unable to invest in stocks, bonds, and real estate, and save significant amounts of money. The student loan crisis in the United States, for instance, stifles any capacity a young person or family might otherwise have to save money, invest, and open a retirement account. 42% of young workers between the ages of 18 and 29 in the United States do not have savings accounts.[116] Where there is abject poverty, any knowledge acquired in a financial literacy class cannot be applied.

It was established earlier that Muslim nations where Islam is the source of a nation's constitution have a tendency to prohibit young girls from pursuing certain career paths or from getting an education altogether. Such nations are to be contrasted with nations, Muslim or otherwise, that do not allow prohibitions on education. Recall that in Afghanistan, women with higher education had better employment opportunities and thus, lower unemployment rates, so what follows is a roadmap the Afghani government can follow in order to lift more women above the poverty line. Gender gaps with respect to education are declining in Middle Eastern and North African nations that have secularized governments, e.g. Egypt, United Arab Emirates. In Arab countries, for

---

[116] Adamczyk, Alicia. "25% of US adults have no retirement savings". *CNBC*. 24 Mar 2019. Web. <https://www.cnbc.com/2019/05/24/25-percent-of-us-adults-have-no-retirement-savings-fed-finds.html>

instance, substantial investments in education have eliminated the gap in some areas by improving women's capacity to be productive in the workforce. Women's secondary school enrollment has increased dramatically since 1960 in nations throughout Southeast Asia. In Southeast Asian, more so than in Arab nations, women have accounted for gradually increasing proportions of total workforce growth.[117]

Studies in these regions also revealed that there is a positive correlation between higher education and decreased susceptibility to domestic abuse. There is, however, a negative correlation between higher education and gender-based income inequality.[118] The speculation in that regard is that Islamic gender norms may explain this anomaly. Higher education may not have resulted in income parity between men and women in Muslim nations, but it has helped to alleviate instances of domestic

---

[117] Offenhauer, Priscilla. "Women In Islamic Societies:A Selected Review of Social Scientific Literature. *Library of Congress*. Nov 2005. Web. <https://www.loc.gov/rr/frd/pdf-files/Women_Islamic_Societies.pdf>

[118] Ibid.

violence. Therefore, the case against prohibiting young girls from pursuing an education has proven tenable. In Afghanistan's case, the gender norms do not appear to have the same effect and as such, following the example of neighboring countries and countries in Northern African will result in lifting more women out of poverty.

    Ultimately, what can be done about issues underlying the decision to terminate pregnancy results in a monumental and daunting task. A single individual is unfit to handle this task and so what is required is a coalition of people who want to combat poverty, deter and prosecute domestic violence, implement better sex education and financial literacy curriculums, and address systemic inequality within their societies. The people within this coalition must be willing to engage one another, for purposes of sharing ideas, improving strategies, and deciding on actionable solutions to the problems women and their families are confronting. The issue here is that nationalistic or patriotic attitudes might impede crowdsourced knowledge of this sort because a proud nation may be reluctant to rely on the insights of another country. As has been made abundantly clear, however, no one nation has risen to the occasion. Some nations and regions have done exceptional jobs in some areas while falling short in others, so the call to share ideas within this coalition cannot be ignored.

4

Why The Debate is Irrelevant: Pro-Life, Pro-Choice, and a Synthesis

If one is a pro-choicer, one is likely accustomed to hearing the worst arguments pro-lifers have to offer. In some cases, arguments are not offered. Their convictions are merely repeated, e.g. life begins at conception; abortion is the killing or murder of an innocent human being. Usually, no effort is made to justify these convictions. Of the arguments that pro-lifers could present, only one of the following arguments is commonly used. Given its common usage and given that I find it to be the weakest argument a pro-lifer can use, I will summarize it first. That will then be followed by arguments that I deem stronger. The arguments themselves are actual arguments put forth by knowledgeable pro-lifers who actually engage with the arguments offered by their opponents. The order in which the arguments will appear is in accordance with their degree of strength. Anyone is welcome to disagree with their order since, though I have thought about the arguments carefully, their degrees of strength is still a matter of opinion.

    The most common argument pro-lifers put forth is an argument rooted in Francis Beckwith's shared-value argument. The thought experiment can be summarized thusly. Suppose you have an uncle, named Jed, who fell into a coma after a car accident. Imagine then that he awakes after two years of being in a coma. With the exception of weight loss, he appears to be the Jed you remember. During his coma, did he retain his intrinsic value as a person? Is it possible the physicians could have killed Jed while he was in a coma — when he was not functioning and behaving normally? If one holds that intrinsic value is contingent on capacities that are immediately exercisable, it is difficult to argue that it would not have bee wrong to kill Jed while he remained in a coma. Yet it would be wrong, Beckwith argues, because he remains the same despite not displaying the qualities that make him the Jed you're familiar with.

As a consequence, one who disagrees with Beckwith's conclusion cannot reply by arguing that because Jed functioned as an intrinsically valuable human being and that since he probably will do so in the future, his life retained its intrinsic value during his coma. For one can instead imagine that when Jed awakens from the coma, he lost virtually all his memories, language capacities, and his ability to engage in rational thinking. He would therefore be the equivalent of a fetus. He would be as he was before he had a past. He would simply have to develop and re-learn these basic capacities as he did as a child in hopes of restoring such capacities in full.[119]

Beckwith's "Uncle Jed" example has been used, albeit not always directly. There are also variants to this argument. Pro-lifers may bring up similar thought-experiments that replace Uncle Jed with a person that is asleep or with craniopagus conjoined twins. The strength of this argument might be

---

[119] Wilcox, Clinton. "Arguments Against Fetal Personhood." *Secular Pro-Life Perspectives*. 4 Feb 2013. Web. 21 Nov 2014.

obvious to any pro-lifer; rather than asking pro-lifers to consider the weaknesses of the argument, they should think about why the following arguments are stronger.

However, prior to moving on to other arguments against abortion, it is necessary to touch on a common variant of Beckwith's shared-value argument, namely any argument that attempts to make abortion and infanticide analogous. This argument follows from Paul Ramsey who argued that there is not an argument in favor of abortion that does not work in favor of infanticide.[120] This argument is a shared-value argument because it assumes that fetuses and infants share properties in common. In the next chapter, I will attempt to demarcate infants from fetuses because they are distinct in one crucial respect.

It can be argued that the next two arguments have the same degree of strength. I, therefore, do not place them in any particular order. The first of the

---

[120] Chapman, Stephan. "From Abortion to Infanticide". *Chicago Tribune*. 22 Apr 1982. Web. 21 Nov 2014.

two I want to summarize is Don Marquis' "Future-Like-Ours" argument. He argues that losing one's life deprives one of every experience one otherwise would have had. It follows then that killing someone is wrong because the victim loses much more than their life. Killing someone, in the biological sense, is not always wrong, but if you killed someone, particularly when they are far from the maximum age of life expectancy, you deprive them of their current values and whatever values they may have in the future. The loss of their future is ultimately what makes killing adult human beings wrong.[121]

Marquis is arguing that all that is necessary is that we find a shared property between adult persons and fetuses. If this property is found, then we can confer rights on the fetus. That property is that a fetus has a future that resembles ours. This argument can be considered a variant of Beckwith's shared-value argument since it also rests on values purportedly shared by adults and fetuses.

---

[121] Marquis, Don. "Why Abortion is Immoral". *Journal of Philosophy, Vol. 86*, pp. 183-202. 1989. Print.

The next argument I want to focus on is what Earl Connee refers to as the Non-Reductionist conclusion. This view was first expressed by Derek Parfit. The Non-Reductionist conclusion follows from his argument, which can be summarized as follows. There is a clear moment when a one began to exist. Parfit considers it implausible to think the moment of one's birth qualifies as this moment. He also does not think a line can be determined during pregnancy. Therefore, life begins at conception. On the Non-Reductionist view, it is the case that every part of one's life is equal parts compromising one's life. So killing a fetus is equivalent to killing an innocent person. It follows from this that all induced abortions are morally wrong; the lone exception, for Parfit, is those that save the mother's life.[122]

This view is non-reductionist because it does not reduce our personhood or humanity to functions, particularly brain functions. It is based on the metaphysical proposition that our substance is

---

[122] Connee, Earl. "Metaphysics and the Morality of Abortion". Mind 108 (432) (1998): 619-646. Print.

pivotal to our identity. This conclusion is in keeping with religious belief in the soul

Since they are contrasted in Connee's paper, I will go on a relevant tangent to touch on the Reductionist conclusion—which is a pro-choice argument. The Reductionist conclusion stems from the Reductionist argument which could be stated as follows:

On the Reductionist View, we do not believe that at every moment I either do or don't exist. We can now deny that a fertilized ovum is a person or human being. ... [The] transition takes time, and is a matter of degree ... We can then plausibly take a different view about the morality of abortion. We can believe that there is nothing wrong with an early abortion, but that it would be seriously wrong to abort a child near the end of a pregnancy ... The cases in between can be treated as matters of degree. The fertilized ovum is not at first, but slowly becomes, a human being and a person. In the same way, the destruction of this organism is not at first but slowly becomes seriously wrong.[123]

---

[123] Ibid.

This argument rests on the non-ambiguity of a fetus' moral status. Since I want this tangent to be brief, I will return to how this is established. Furthermore, I will attach the argument from the ambiguity of a fetus' moral status, since it is germane to the discussion.

The last argument in favor of the pro-life position, which is, in my opinion, the strongest, is the argument from potentiality. This argument is arguably best defended by Reginald William. He states the following: "If all things being equal, the more valuable something is, the more we tend to condemn deliberately preventing its existence, it is also natural to think that when something is of but slight or modest value, we would not condemn just any deliberate act that ends up preventing its existence. It is plausible to think that, in such an instance, we would only condemn a deliberate act that results in there not being something which itself stood to engender the relevant object of value."[124]

---

[124] William, Reginald. "Abortion, Potential, and Value". Cambridge University Press. Utilitas Volume 20 Issue 02 June 2008, pp 169-186. Print.

The above is a clear statement of the argument from potential. William gives us several examples, e.g. the seed and food, arguing not only from potential but also from the value of the thing preceding that which we deem valuable. The reason this argument has the highest degree of strength is that it is compelling and likely the most philosophically sound point that can be made. William tells us the following about people who encounter this argument: "Yet many people who encounter these criticisms, including Grade-A philosophy students and bona fide philosophers, end up endorsing the argument from potential at the end of the day."[125] This is not surprising since strong arguments are usually convincing and/or difficult to grapple with. In other words, even them who disagree with this argument have to think carefully; their reasoning has to be clearer if they are to refute the argument. This is not always obvious, so acceptance can follow; if not, one might opt to remain agnostic on a given matter.

---

[125] Ibid.

The above serves as a summary of the best pro-life arguments. In fact, these are the arguments that should commonly be heard. Unfortunately, what one usually gets is the poisoning of the well, false analogies, e.g. abortion is murder, ad hominem, and appeal to emotion. Aside from misrepresenting pro-choicers and the case they are making, pro-lifers are also damaging their own case. If any pro-lifer fails to see the strength the above arguments have over the usual mantras, propaganda, and outright lies put forth by some pro-lifers, it is a failure in reason. The arguments above are not only stronger, but they are more conducive to the discussion. One will get further in a discussion on abortion if one chooses to present one or more of these arguments rather than marginalizing one's opponents and making sweeping generalizations about them.

With that said, let us return to the Reductionist conclusion and the points used to support the argument. McMahon argued that a fetus becomes a person at the onset of brainwaves. Given this, it can be said that the Reductionist conclusion is also a progressive conclusion since the argument attempts to show a clear path from non-person to person. McMahon isn't the only person to argue this. Michael Gazzaniga states the following:

> Clearly, I believe that a fertilized egg, a clump of cells with no brain, is hardly deserving of the same moral status we confer on the newborn child or the functioning adult. Mere possession of the genetic material for a future human being does not make a human being. The developing embryo that becomes a fetus that becomes a baby is the product of a dynamic interaction with its environment in the womb, its postnatal experiences, and a host of other factors. A purely genetic description of the human species does not describe a human being. *A human being represents a whole other level of organization, as distinct from a simple embryo as an embryo is distinct from an egg and sperm.* It is the dynamics between genes and environment that make a human being. Indeed, most of us are willing to grant this special status to a developing entity long before it is born, but surely not before the entity even has a brain.[126]

---

[126] Gazzaniga, Michael. "The Ethical Brain". *The Dana Foundation*. 1 Jul 2005. Web. 21 Nov 2014.

I placed particular emphasis because that statement, in particular, demonstrates how there is an underlying progression in the Reductionist Conclusion. Toward the end, he speaks of granting this special status to fetuses before birth; however, he states that we can't grant them this status before they have brains. Another iteration was offered by Gertler who proposed 22-24 weeks gestation because this is when the neocortex begins producing EEG waves. Inherent in his proposal is the view that human cognition is when cognitive capability begins and is therefore when personhood should be protected. Similarly, Burgess and Tawia defined the functioning brain as one showing activity similar to the activity in adult brains. They posit that a critical minimum level of structural organization is required, with functional components that are developed enough to perform. They therefore conclude that a fetus becomes conscious at 32-36 weeks gestation.[127]

---

[127] Jones, D Gareth. "The Problematic Symmetry Between Brain Birth and Brain Death". *Journal of Medical Ethic Issue 24*:237-242. 1998. Print.

The Reductionist conclusion is therefore the result of an argument stating that personhood reduces to brain function. This is what is meant by the non-ambiguity of a fetus' moral status. Its status is not ambiguous since we can demarcate, on the basis of empirical conclusions, between a person and a non-person and therefore, between a fetus and a fully developed human being.

Pro-choicers who are unaware of these empirical conclusions can argue from the presumed ambiguity of the fetus' moral status. They can argue that since we cannot establish whether or not a fetus is a person, it is best to side with precaution. Using this reasoning, Nathan Nabis offers his Precautionary Principle:

When dealing with a decision between the freedoms of choice and consciousness belonging to an actual woman as opposed to the uncertain moral status of a fetus gestating in her body, the most cautious option is to honor the physical and mental integrity of the woman and her best judgments regarding her own interests. This position requires the least amount of comprehensive assumptions.[128]

    The Precautionary Principe, even in light of the fact that we can establish personhood, is compelling. Even if we agree that a fetus is a person, it is a very peculiar kind of person since its gestating the body of another person. If bodily autonomy is a chief unalienable right, then the right to choose should remain a legal option. This is closely related to what is arguably the strongest argument for the pro-choice position—the argument from bodily autonomy.

    The argument from autonomy can, but does not have to, follow from the Precautionary Principle. Torcello argues "that where moral uncertainty is a factor, a society is not justified in enacting oppressive legislation that encroaches on the physical and mental autonomy to which free and equal citizens otherwise have a right in a just liberal society."[129] In

---

[128] Torcello, Lawrence. "A Precautionary Tale: Separating the Infant from the Fetus." *Res Publica Issue 15*: 17–31. 2009. Print.

[129] Ibid.

other words, if the moral status of the fetus is uncertain, a government cannot infringe on a woman's right to bodily autonomy.

Where it doesn't follow from the Precautionary Principle, one could refer to Margaret Olivia Little who stated that "a person's right to life is circumscribed at the point at which that life involves occupying and using another's body."[130] Or one could also cite Susan Sherwin who "argues that pregnant women can justifiably refuse to view their fetus as having full moral standing because of the ontological dependence of the fetus on the pregnant woman. The fetus would not even exist without this unique and intimate dependency on the pregnant woman."[131]

Pro-choicers are not to be let off the hook because it can be qualified that some pro-choicers have not adequately distinguished their view from one that solely favors abortion. It has been repeated throughout this work that reducing abortion rates is a

---

[130] Kaposy, Chris. "Proof and Persuasion in the Philosophical Debate about Abortion." *Philosophy and Rhetoric Volume 43, Number 2*: pp. 139-162. 2010. Print.

[131] Ibid.

worthwhile goal and despite the exhaustive presentation thus far, the question of why is it a worthwhile goal may linger. Think again about the women who typically have abortions. If it is the case that there are far less expensive ways to avoid getting pregnant, then one must ask why she does not seem to know her options or, as has been established in regions where abortion is prohibited, why she lacks access to contraceptives. Bear in mind also that even in nations where abortion is legal, procedures are not always funded by the government and so, the costs associated with these procedures are sometimes paid out of pocket since health insurance does not always cover the costs, either partially or in full.

So when pro-lifers refer to some pro-choicers as "pro-aborts," the pro-choicer should identify the source of that misnomer. Pro-choicers do not always care to discuss contraceptives — which should serve as the primary resort for anyone looking to avoid getting pregnant. From a practical standpoint, there is little sense in opting to endure hormonal changes, morning sickness, and other complications if the woman in question simply avoid an unwanted pregnancy altogether by opting to take birth control, getting an IUD procedure, convincing her partner to get a vasectomy, or using condoms. In a country like the United States, for example, government funding for abortion is not supported when a Republican holds the office of President. So unless a woman's insurance covers the cost of the abortion procedure, she may pay upwards of $450 to terminate pregnancy. Again, there is no practical need to go that far if a couple can purchase a pack of condoms where each condom costs an average of $1. With all these factors considered, reducing abortion rates is indeed a worthwhile goal.

What remains after the armistice is a call to action. Rather than being pro-life or pro-choice and debating one another endlessly, I encourage everyone to meet at the common ground, to be pro-active. Too many people on all sides have been content with debating one another for recognition or vainglory. For purposes of securing equality for impoverished families, it is imperative to take action. Bear in mind that a lot of women who have abortions do not want to end their pregnancies. There should be an effort to close income gaps between affluent and poor women. The problem is not abortion itself, but rather what underlies the decision to have an abortion — income inequality and any racial and cultural drivers precipitating it, poverty, domestic abuse, and the lack of educational and employment opportunities. What is needed is a coalition willing to solve these issues.

5
Why A Fetus is Not a Person and Should Not Have Legal Rights

The abortion debate does not retain significance even when discussing the hypothetical personhood of a fetus. The more skeptical reader has probably wondered why I support this conclusion. For sake of clarification and not of argument, I will now present reasons as to why the discussion is unimportant. There should not be a delay in action given the assumption that a fetus is a person, potential or actual. Discussions of the sort not only delay or impede action but also guarantee the dissolution of any productive dialogue that might have been had. Individuals who participate in such discussions often come away angry, fully decided on the notion that their opponent holds an inhumane perspective. While such a conclusion is an exaggeration, regardless of which party is making the accusation, one can begin to see why it is worthwhile to demonstrate why this particular aspect of the abortion debate is not important. The hope is that what follows proves persuasive.

Given that the Argument From Fetal Personhood follows from a distinction found in Aristotle's metaphysics, the presentation that follows must be prefaced with the basic knowledge concerning the distinction of potentiality and actuality. A simple example will illuminate the distinction so that one is not bogged down by the confusion even some philosophers deal with when confronted by the distinction. The raw material in a manufacturing plant is potentially a plane, car, or train, among a number of other things. For Aristotle, the raw material is the matter or the potentiality that compromises the substance, form, or the actuality. Confusion sets in when delving into the priority Aristotle gives actuality over potentiality. Since an egg is potentially a chicken, one might conclude that, temporally speaking, the egg precedes the chicken. Per Aristotle, however, since the egg is identical to the species that existed before it, the chicken precedes the egg. One can see how this easily applies to human fetuses and developed human beings, but just like raw materials are not identical to the planes and automobiles built from them, a human fetus is not identical to a developed human being. This was already established in the previous chapter, but for those who remain unconvinced, what follows is a more exhaustive treatment of the distinction between fetuses and human persons.

Purposeful Modification

Kevin Tobia, a Graduate student at Yale University, speaks about a self emerging from change rather than the typical self people speak of, namely the self that persists despite change.[132] Purposeful change involves change resulting in self-discovery or becoming a better version of oneself, be it socially, morally, with respect to one's career or passions, and so on.

---

[132] Tobias, Kevin. "Change Becomes You." *Aeon*. 19 Sept 2017. Web. <https://aeon.co/amp/essays/to-be-true-to-ones-self-means-changing-to-become-that-self?utm_content=buffer99845&utm_medium=social&utm_source=facebook.com&utm_campaign=buffer>

With that in mind, I think Tobia has, perhaps inadvertently, identified the stark contrast between even infants and fetuses, and has thus tilted the scales in favor of the pro-choice position. Fetuses cannot and do not purposefully change or modify themselves, and that is mainly because they do not exist *independently in the world*, i.e. in society, and therefore, do not have access to the experiences and sensations serving as the impetus for such change. Newborns, on the other hand, can and do purposefully change and modify simply because they do have access to the sensations and experiences in the world. There is also the fact that the parents and relatives of the newborn have expectations of the kind of purposeful changes they have already observed in themselves and other people they know, and they can thus extrapolate from such experiences and have similar expectations of their newborn.

This definitely sets aside Singer's argument for infanticide because Tobia has identified a clear demarcator between fetuses and newborns. Purposeful modification is the key component of personhood. What makes for a person is the fact that people self-modify. People, specifically in the absence of psychological or cognitive issues, are concerned with improving themselves. They are concerned with being better socially. The average teenager, for instance, has insecurities and awkward quirks, many of which they foresee overcoming as adults.

Interestingly, Tobia's purposeful modification is also a defeater for Marquis' Future-Like-Ours Argument. A fetus cannot purposely modify because it has not developed the cognitive capacities to do so. It is also not an active participant in the world, which is to say society, the realm of laws. While an infant does not yet possess the capacity to purposely modify all its own, a commonly held assumption by parents is that it will develop in the same way they did, in the same way their other children have, and as such, they purposely modify on its behalf by nurturing the infant so that it develops accordingly. An infant can have a future like ours *iff* it possesses the substratum for basic cognitive functions and if a caretaker purposely modifies on its behalf until the point at which she is a mature enough child to want certain commodities and experiences, and has goals that she intends to reach.

Ultimately, Tobia has identified the key component of personhood. In fact, it is both necessary and sufficient to adequately define what is meant by a human person. Of course, it goes beyond biology and genetics. It is not enough that a human person is genetically human and related to its parents. There is more that constitutes a person and *purposeful modification* is clearly the most important qualifier of what a person is. This is precisely why fetuses are not persons and are thus exempt from the legal rights reserved for persons. They are most certainly exempt from receiving these rights because they cannot receive such rights over and above the would-be mother who has a demonstrable propensity for purposeful modification. That of course leads us into the well-established Argument from Bodily Autonomy, but an argument from purposeful modification is clearly sufficient to dispense with the Argument From Fetal Personhood. Fetuses are no doubt genetically human, but they are not one and the same with a human person, and that is because they cannot and do not have the capacity for purposeful modification. While purposeful modification is a clear defeater for the Argument From Fetal Personhood, there is still more to be said about the genetic and biological dimensions involved in this discussion.

From Potentiality to Actuality

Pro-lifers tend to give human beings an undue special status all while ignoring human evolution. Human potential or more specifically, *homo sapien* potential would not exist without an ancestor's (probably *homo antecessor*) potential. Furthermore, *homo sapien* potential would not have been realized without the actuality of ancestors and likewise, without the divergence of ancestors, great apes would not have progressed as they have. We share about 98.5% DNA with chimpanzees and some 96% with gorillas, two facts that establish a common ancestry. So this special status pro-lifers assign to humans is more actually an example of *special pleading* because it is not at all clear why chimps and gorillas do not qualify for such status; also, neanderthals, given what we currently know about them, are in many respects like *homo sapiens* (a fact that made their interbreeding possible) and as such, would qualify for such status without question.[133] Yet on the pro-life view, no human ancestor qualifies for this status, an attitude that should strike one as suspicious.

    Human evolution, like evolution *in toto*, has an underlying genetic component that explains these variations in populations over time. That same genetic component continues among all populations of species and thus, better explains how potentiality results in actuality. Furthermore, to avoid thoroughly metaphysical language, potential is not non-natural or supernatural, but rather a statistically predictable

---

[133] Sample, Ian. "Neanderthals – not modern humans – were first artists on Earth, experts claim". *The Guardian*. 22 Feb 2018. Web. <https://www.theguardian.com/science/2018/feb/22/neanderthals-not-humans-were-first-artists-on-earth-experts-claim>

pattern present in the genome of an organism. The pattern is so predictable that one can readily explain how and why that which is formless becomes something with form.

What follows is a brief overview showing how the actuality of parents results in the potentiality and probable actuality of a child. It is also important to note that given genetics, there are a number of factors that determine morphological sex, eye color, hair color, skin tone, and so on. With that in mind, imagine that in universe A, Jack and Jill have a baby girl named Janice and that in universe B, they have a boy named Jake. Let us also consider the important differences in each child, differences that explain why Janice exists in A and Jake in B.

In universe A, Jack and Jill are both 24-years-old when they agree to have a child. Jack and Jill are wealthy and have spent the last four years of their relationship traveling. Neither of them is stressed and have no trouble being happy and grateful for all that they have. When considering that high stress increases the probability of having a boy, it is no surprise that Jill gives birth to Janice nine months later.[134] Yet that still does not explain why Janice has brown eyes (though *both* her parents have blue eyes), her mother's hair color, and her father's hitchhiker thumb. In the main, had another sperm fertilized the egg, Janice very likely would have been born with completely different features. Despite low stress levels, there is also the fact that Jack has five sisters and no brothers, therefore increasing the probability of having a girl.[135] This still does not explain why Janice has brown rather than blue eyes, blonde rather than brown hair, and a hitchhiker thumb rather than a straight thumb.

Allelic combination is important in explaining Janice's phenotypic features. Should both parents pass on recessive genes, Janice is born with a hitchhiker thumb. Or alternatively, if there is a combination of dominant and recessive genes, she

---

[134] NA. "Can Stress Determine Your Baby's Gender?". *The Week*. 18 Oct 2011. Web. <https://theweek.com/articles/480919/stress-determine-babys-gender>

[135] NA. "Boy or girl? It's in the father's genes". *Newcastle University*. 11 Dec 2017. Web. <https://www.ncl.ac.uk/press/articles/archive/2015/08/boyorgirlitsinthefathersgenes.html>

may have a chance to have a hitchhiker thumb or a straight thumb. If there is a combination of dominant genes, then she will predictably have a straight thumb.[136] Eye color tends to be similar, albeit more complicated.

For instance, the assumption is that since Janice's parents have blue eyes, she will also have blue eyes. There are two genes integral to determine eye pigmentation: OCA2 and HERC2. An active HERC2 activates OCA2, which determines pigment; given this, we know that this is what explains Janice's brown eyes. Her counterpart in universe B, Jake, has either a broken HERC2 or a broken OCA2 and therefore, has blue eyes.[137] He also has brown hair and a straight thumb. He has a straight thumb because instead of a recessive and dominant gene (what we find in Janice's genome), we find two

---

[136] NA. "What is Hitchhiker's Thumb?". *Health Hema*. 20 Feb 2018. Web. <https://healthhema.com/hitchhikers-thumb/>

[137] Starr, Barry. "How Blue Eyed Parents Can Have Brown Eyed Children". *The Tech*. 27 Jul 2012. Web. <https://genetics.thetech.org/how-blue-eyed-parents-can-have-brown-eyed-children>

dominant genes in Jake's genome. Their disparate hair colors are explained in this manner as well.

Form, likewise, follows suit. Drosophilae have been crucial in experiments in evolutionary biology and genetics. In observing curious mutations in these flies, geneticists discovered homeotic genes (Hox) that determine the body pattern of all organisms. Hox genes themselves come from a Hox-like ancestor that explains the similarities Hox genes have from organism to organism.[138] Hox genes direct the process of forming the heads of organisms from mice to humans, and the proteins associated with the gene ensure that structures develop in the area of the body they pertain to. Simply put, the proteins encode specified attributes related to position and so the arm of a human forms where one expects it to rather than in another position on the body. Predictably, limb malformations result from deletion of chromosomes across Hox genes. The graphic below shows an evolutionary tree for Hox-like genes:

---

[138] NA. "Homeotic Genes and Body Patterns". *Teach.Genetics*. ND. Web. <https://learn.genetics.utah.edu/content/basics/hoxgenes/>

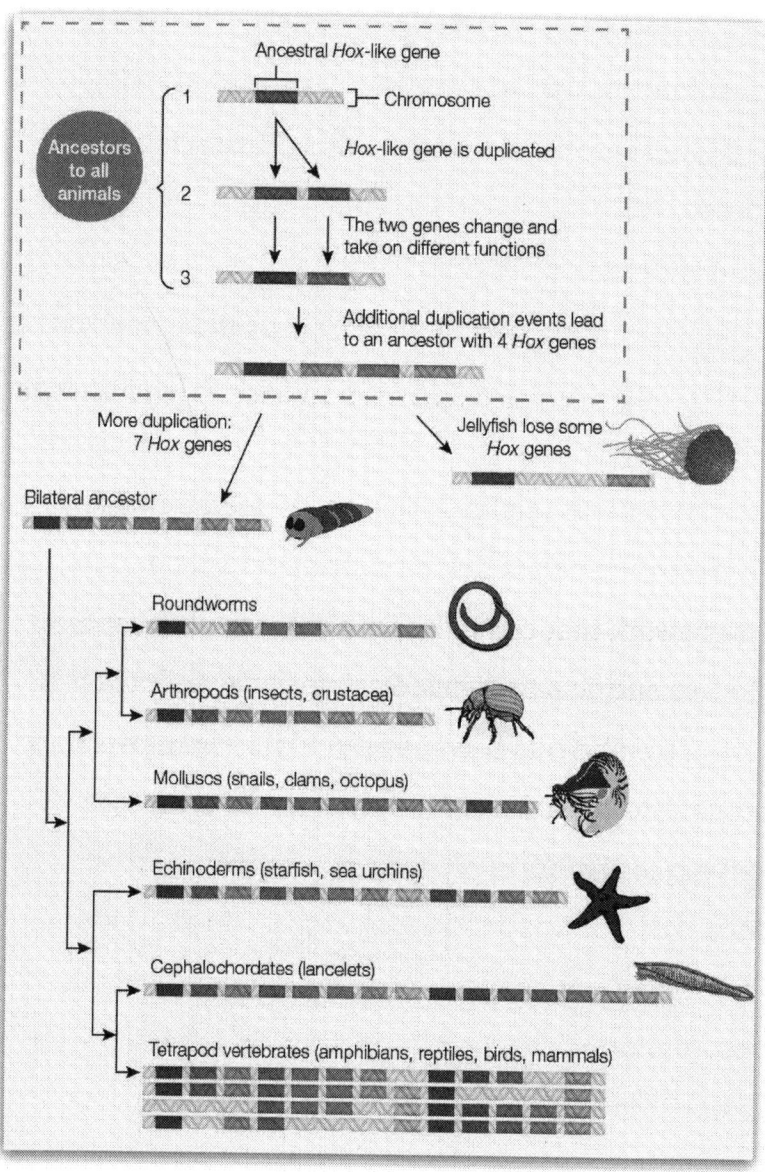

[139] Ibid. [93]

There is an evolutionary and genetic history that informs how a comparatively formless embryo develops into a human being. There are also traits that are arbitrary as there is no purpose as to why someone would have brown rather than blue eyes or a hitchhiker thumb rather than a straight thumb. Some traits are inconsequential with respect to who a given person is.

What is required is either no metaphysical framework at all (à la logical positivists) or a framework that coincides with modern philosophical and scientific paradigms. Despite the potential for a human embryo to become an actual human person, a roughly predictable, naturalistic set of occurrences take place before every human birth. The process is also a fragile one as an injury to the would-be mother can end the pregnancy; genetic anomalies and implantation anywhere other than the uterus can make it so that this potentiality never results in an actuality. None of the preferred metaphysical systems that pro-lifers employ explain the fragility of this process not just in humans, but in other organisms as well. It should therefore be clear that there is no need to go down a metaphysical rabbit hole.

Abortion is Not Murder

Consider the following argument by Bill Vallicella:

P1 Murder should be illegal
P2 Abortion is murder
C Ergo, abortion should be illegal.[140]

Even if one were to grant the undeniable personhood of a fetus, there is still the issue that the intentional killing of this person does not constitute a murder. The pivotal error pro-choicers make is that they tend to define abortion and ignore what it is being equated

---

[140] Vallicella, Bill. "Can One Reasonably Hold that Abortion is Murder but Ought to be Legal?". *Maverick Philosopher*. 7 Oct 2018. Web. <https://maverickphilosopher.typepad.com/maverick_philosopher/2018/10/can-one-reasonably-hold-that-abortion-is-murder-but-ought-to-be-legal.html?fbclid=IwAR2qNTwvMMRqYg44Dk1rsIklavUsJ6CfLV0ED5VMIek3JIAoJzlmmuO1NGY>

to. They should also consider the *legal* definition of murder, since Vallicella is alluding to the legal rather than the moral definition.

The killing of an embryo or fetus is done with intentions and motives altogether different from those underlying homicide, and as such, from a legal standpoint, it cannot be approached as murder or even a lesser offense like manslaughter. There is no degree of murder applicable to abortion; the intention and motive are not the same either, so even from a legal perspective, abortion is not murder. It would constitute an intentional killing of a different sort, of an even benevolent sort. Therefore, a woman who has an abortion cannot be tried and convicted as a murderer, neither can the doctor who performed the abortion. This also serves as an indictment of any country that continues to criminalize abortion.

Let us consider first-degree murder. Premeditation is already an issue for Vallicella's argument; the prosecution would not be able to argue that the mother had a malicious intent to kill this person. As for second degree, even though lacking the premeditation criterion, implies a reckless disregard for human life. The prosecution cannot accuse a woman of that either. What is more is that, if pro-lifers were right in that a fetus is a person despite its viability, then restrictive policies would be the only choice we would have. Like Vallicella's argument implies, murder is treated in an extremely restrictive manner; even self-defense has to be established with no room for doubt.

So if abortion were murder, it would be dealt with in like manner. So setting metaphysics and ethics aside, from a practical point of view, we should be wary of equating abortion with murder because the latter has been dealt with in a restrictive manner and it should be clear now that there are better ways of addressing it, especially given the deadly consequences of such policies, policies that have received thorough treatment in previous chapters. So even if for solely practical reasons, we should shy from such equivalence *even if* it could be proven that abortion is murder. The issue here is that no pro-lifer has qualified that statement in any manner that does not make for a bare assertion. Abortion is simply not murder and to think of women who have abortions as murderers is to misunderstand this issue altogether. What should be addressed are the common motivations for seeking an abortion, poverty and its correlates (e.g. lack of employment opportunities, high infant and maternal mortality rates) and domestic violence, most especially. Ways to address these issues have received sufficient treatment in this work, so there is no room left to excuse apathy as it regards these issues.

      Therefore, since a non-viable fetus is not a person, pro-lifers cannot demand rights to be conferred onto them. Moreover, the legal rights of one person should not come at the expense of another person, since all that does is perpetuate injustice. What's crucial in this particular case is that the hypothetical but demonstrably unfounded personhood of fetuses does not take priority over the undeniable and demonstrable personhood of women. The legal rights of hypothetical persons also cannot take priority over those of established persons. It follows from this that embryos and non-viable fetuses are not persons on whom legal rights should be conferred.

Conclusion

Now we can return to one of the central questions of this work — whether the abortion debate really matters. It should be clear given the discussion thus far that it does not matter, specifically not more so than the factors that result in women choosing to terminate their pregnancies. In arguing about the politics and ethics of abortion, people have lost track of something crucial. Whether the intention is to mitigate or to put an end to something, the focus should be on the underlying factors. Sure, pro-lifers and pro-choicers cannot find much common ground. Common ground is not impossible to find notwithstanding. I am not alone in seeing that reducing abortion is a goal all sides should pursue. Pro-lifers may continue to contend that they would rather put an end to abortion. I will stress, once again, that in order to reduce or put an end to something, the same steps have to be taken. This is common ground, elusive no more!

I will also reiterate that I do not have to agree with a pro-lifer's reasons for wanting to put an end to abortion. I only have to agree with them in concluding that targeting the precursors of abortion is a valuable endeavor in and of itself. The decision to have an abortion is due to a variety of reasons, many of which were discussed at great length. To reiterate, among these reasons are the fact that the woman cannot afford to raise a child or in some cases, another child, having a baby would dramatically alter her life, or she does not want to be a single mom or continue to experience domestic abuse — as was discussed in the first two chapters. The first of these reasons is important because it leads to a problem people, whether pro-lifer or pro-choicer, should be concerned about: poverty. The poverty rates for women and children discussed in the first chapter are cause for concern. If so many children are currently in poverty it cannot be expected that the mothers of those children will want to continue a new pregnancy in all cases. It is only reasonable that some of them will choose to terminate the pregnancy.

This leads, of course, to another issue worth addressing. If one cannot afford a child at the moment, one should do everything in one's power to prevent pregnancy in the first place. As statistics have shown abortion rates are higher among younger women. It was also demonstrated that this entails an educational or literacy problem. Better sex education curriculums are necessary. Contraception needs to be available so that abortion rates continue to decrease. Access to reproductive healthcare needs to be available as well. This is a reasonable goal no matter what one's personal motives are.

Then there is the issue of relationship issues, specifically domestic violence and reproductive coercion. We cannot expect a woman to willingly carry the child of an abusive significant other. Given that this is a problem according to data one year after another, as observed in the second chapter, domestic violence should receive a lot more attention. This is, no doubt, more difficult to address than the issue of poverty. Providing accurate sex education is one thing, but convincing abusive men that abuse is wrong seems to be a more daunting task. As was explained, abusive men are not made overnight. It was established that there is likely something that needs to be addressed in overall male psychology. This entails taking therapeutic measures that are not always made available to perpetrators of abuse. Regardless, this is something worth taking the time to figure out.

This is why I have concluded that the abortion debate does not matter as much as some people think it does. The moral status of a fetus, potentiality, shared value, reductionism, and non-reductionism are distractions obscuring the real issues underlying the decision to terminate pregnancy. Limiting abortion by focusing on its precursors is a worthwhile goal. Whether one sees it as a worthwhile goal because of its inherent value, as my argument in the previous chapter attempted to show, or because one desires to put an end to abortion does not matter. In other words, one's religious, political, or personal motives for wanting to act against the precursors of abortion makes no difference. This is how to finally synthesize two antithetical positions. This is the common ground that has proven elusive for decades. Reducing abortion is periphery when considering male psychology and domestic abuse, poverty, lack of jobs, and sex education or sex illiteracy. What will result in lasting change is actionable strategies to alleviate the issues confronting women choosing to terminate their pregnancies. Quality of life will improve for families, abortion rates will be reduced, and more importantly, babies will be born into self-sufficient households rather than into abject poverty. The arguments, whether for or against abortion, are entirely secondary when these issues are considered.

 The hope is that this is now salient. The hope is that the debate has now been put to rest. While dissuading someone of their current view might give one a sense of personal fulfillment, it does nothing for women and children in poverty; it does nothing for perpetrators and victims of domestic abuse. While convincing someone of the strength of one's convictions go a long way in reaffirming these convictions in one's mind, that ultimately accomplishes nothing. Nowhere is this debate more pronounced than it is in the United States and I think the reason for that is obvious. The emphasis the country places on individualism results in an egoism that pervades every corner of American culture. Why someone votes for who they vote for or identifies with a certain political or religious group narrows down to this base individualism.

As such, the majority of people who take part in the abortion debate, despite any moral grandstanding, are in it for themselves. A pro-lifer, for instance, cannot possibly care about the life of a hypothetical person yet to be born if they are overlooking the undeniable personhood of the woman struggling with the decision to terminate her pregnancy. On the flip side, a pro-choicer cannot possibly care about options if they do not say enough about contraception, improved sex education curriculum, economic inequality, and related issues surrounding the decision to have an abortion. In effect then, none of the participants in this debate are thinking of others. They are in pursuit of confirmation for their prized perspectives or are attempting to find self-gratification in convincing others of their perspectives or debasing the views of their opponents.

I must reiterate therefore that what is needed is a coalition. Pro-lifer and pro-choicer must come together and realize that there is now a common ground that has been clearly identified. While I may have not synthesized these views in the traditional way of taking the best and most functional parts of both and creating a hybrid position, the hope is that I have effectively dissolved both positions by showing the desperate need there is for action. Both sides must agree to an armistice and act now. Poverty will persist without brainstorming and eventual proposals. If people are either complacent or apathetic, these issues may never come to the attention of lawmakers.

What leads to change in a country's laws are its people. Whether via democracy or revolt that overturns a despotic government, it is people and their convictions that make a difference. Pro-lifers and pro-choicers have convictions, but it must be asked to what end have these convictions proven useful. Once abortion is legalized, pro-lifers continue to protest legalization while pro-choicers rejoice in what amounts to a hollow victory. Legalization and decriminalization of abortion is a small step in the right direction, but as this work has shown, there is so much more that needs to be done afterward. Pro-choicers cannot celebrate a woman in poverty having a procedure that costs as much as her gross weekly earnings, a procedure that costs some 40% of her rent, a procedure she is often forced to pay out of pocket. That, once again, does nothing at all to alleviate poverty.

 Pro-choicers in the United States have done a lot to ensure that abortion is safe and legal in many states and yet sex education across the country has stagnated and is grossly inaccurate. It is demonstrably the case, even in vociferous debates, that not enough is said about these issues and not enough is proposed with respect to how to address them. This work attempts to encourage an armistice.

This is a call to action, yes, but it is also a call to do better. If all sides involved are going to continue to engage one another, do so in a meaningful way, in a way that stresses the importance of taking action. Do so in a way that results in organizing and planning in order to inspire lasting change.

    All this is to ask that pro-lifers wholly abandon their position because as this work has made clear, a truly pro-life position will pay closer attention to the quality of life of women and their families, especially the children they already have. Pro-choicers are also being asked to abandon their position because the array of choices women actually have are often not made clear and in far too many cases, women are given an ultimatum: either she is to give birth to a child so that it is born into poverty or terminate her pregnancy. Ultimately, what is being asked of people who truly care about the issues underlying the decision to have an abortion is to begin identifying as pro-action. More importantly, we all need to see the monumental need to take action and follow through so that quality of life is improved for families around the world. Not pro-life. Not pro-choice. Pro-action!

Made in the USA
Middletown, DE
01 June 2021